NIGHT AND HER STARS

BY
RICHARD GREENBERG

DRAMATISTS
PLAY SERVICE
INC.

NIGHT AND HER STARS
Copyright © 1997, Richard Greenberg

ALL RIGHTS RESERVED
CAUTION: Professionals and amateurs are hereby warned that performance of NIGHT AND HER STARS is subject to a royalty. It is fully protected under the copyright laws of the United States of America, and of all countries covered by the International Copyright Union (including the Dominion of Canada and the rest of the British Commonwealth), and of all countries covered by the Pan-American Copyright Convention, the Universal Copyright Convention, the Berne Convention, and of all countries with which the United States has reciprocal copyright relations. All rights, including professional/amateur stage rights, motion picture, recitation, lecturing, public reading, radio broadcasting, television, video or sound recording, all other forms of mechanical or electronic reproduction, such as CD-ROM, CD-I, information storage and retrieval systems and photocopying, and the rights of translation into foreign languages, are strictly reserved. Particular emphasis is placed upon the matter of readings, permission for which must be secured from the Author's agent in writing.

The English language stock and amateur stage performance rights in the United States, its territories, possessions and Canada in NIGHT AND HER STARS are controlled exclusively by the DRAMATISTS PLAY SERVICE, INC., 440 Park Avenue South, New York, N.Y. 10016. No professional or non-professional performance of the Play may be given without obtaining in advance the written permission of the DRAMATISTS PLAY SERVICE, INC., and paying the requisite fee.

Inquiries concerning all other rights should be addressed to George Lane, c/o William Morris Agency, Inc., 1325 Avenue of the Americas, New York, N.Y. 10019.

SPECIAL NOTE
Anyone receiving permission to produce NIGHT AND HER STARS is required (1) to give credit to the Author as sole and exclusive Author of the Play on the title page of all programs distributed in connection with performances of the Play and in all instances in which the title of the Play appears for purposes of advertising, publicizing or otherwise exploiting the Play and/or a production thereof. The name of the Author must appear on a separate line, in which no other name appears, immediately beneath the title and in size of type equal to 50% of the largest, most prominent letter used for the title of the Play. No person, firm or entity may receive credit larger or more prominent than that accorded the Author; and (2) to give the following acknowledgment on the title page of all programs distributed in connection with performances of the Play in size equal to the greater of 50% of the size of the Designers or 10% of the size of the title of the play:

Originally produced in New York
by Manhattan Theatre Club
With funds provided by AT&T: Onstage
on April 26, 1995

Commissioned and first produced
by South Coast Repertory

NIGHT AND HER STARS was produced by Manhattan Theatre Club (Lynne Meadow, Artistic Director; Barry Grove, Managing Director) at The American Place Theatre, in New York City, on April 26, 1995. It was directed by David Warren; the set design was by Derek McLane; the costume design was by Walker Hicklin; the lighting design was by Peter Kaczorowski; the original music and sound design were by Michael Roth and the production stage manager was Ruth Kreshka. The cast was as follows:

HERB STEMPEL .... Patrick Breen
MARK VAN DOREN .... Keith Charles
DAN ENRIGHT .... Peter Frechette
TOBY STEMPEL .... Ileen Getz
AL FREEDMAN .... Jordan Lage
JACK BARRY .... David Andrew MacDonald
WARREN CORSO .... Reese Madigan
DORIS .... Linda Pierce
CHARLES VAN DOREN .... John Slattery
FANS, JOURNALISTS, CONTESTANTS,
CONGRESSPEOPLE, TV PERSONNEL, ETC .... The Company

AUTHOR'S NOTE

A counter-myth is nothing more than the myth someone else believes. *Night and Her Stars* is based in history, has much in common with history, must not be mistaken for history. Facts have been shifted, eliminated, recombined, and invented, according to dramatic need. And while the characters of the play have far too much in common with their (well-known) real world counterparts for changing names to have been an option — it would have seemed a coy gesture — they have been freely imagined and should be considered virtually fictional. In other words, if, after encountering the play, you happen to meet one of the real people, presume nothing.

CHARACTERS

Announcer
Fan One
Fan Two
Fan Three
TV Voice
Young Fan
Dan Enright
Sponsor (Ben)
Al Freedman
Network (Roger)
Jack Barry
Stumped Contestant (Silent)
Another Stumped Contestant (Silent)
Herb Stempel
Toby Stempel
Editorialist
Housewife
Charles Van Doren
Doris
Rabid Fan
Warren Corso
Spats O'Brian
TV Voice (Frank)
Dave Garroway
Stalwart Fan
More Stalwart Fan
Gingerly Fan
Investigator
Radio Voices
Congress One
Congress Two
Congress Three
Congress Four
Congress Five
Mark Van Doren

The first in time and the first in importance of the influences upon the mind is that of nature. Every day, the sun; and after sunset, Night and her stars. Ever the winds blow, ever the grass grows. Every day, men and women, conversing — beholding and beholden. The scholar is he of all men whom this spectacle engages. He must settle its value in his mind. What is nature to him ...

Ralph Waldo Emerson, from *The American Scholar*

NIGHT AND HER STARS

ACT ONE

In darkness.

ANNOUNCER.
... Revlon, the Greatest Name in Cosmetics,
announces:
Living Lipstick —
for the girl who wants to get tender
with the opposite gender.
And now
back to *The Sixty-Four Thousand Dollar Question* ...
(Lights come up on fans as they speak, each before a cove of television lights.)
FAN ONE.
Please win:
I need new wallpaper —
FAN TWO.
Please win:
the mobile air's broken —
FAN THREE.
Please win:
I could use that operation ...
TV VOICE.
I'm sorry,
that's an incorrect answer ...
FAN ONE.
Damn —
FAN TWO.
I'm so disappointed —
FAN THREE.
I expected better ...

(Lights fade on them. Musical chord. A younger Fan appears.)
YOUNG FAN.
What was life like before television?
(Title: The quiz shows are the rage of 1956. Lights: Dan Enright, solo.)
ENRIGHT.
But are we satisfied?
Remember: I was there for radio.
Radio was fine,
but radio, listen:
with radio, there was an out,
a margin for error,
a crack for the imagination.
That was its weakness,
the fatal flaw —
but flaws are for mending
and now we have these Boxes of Light,
Boxes of Light
speeding one vision through the land.
Now when Ma Perkins is on,
she's not "my" Ma Perkins
or "your" Ma Perkins,
she's just, "Ma Perkins" —
the absolute, uncontested, no-room-for-doubt Ma Perkins.
Maybe I'm crazy but that gives me a little thrill.
Now we've had a good run,
I won't say we haven't
with these little quiz things:
with *The Sixty-Four Thousand Dollar Question*,
with *The Sixty-Four Thousand Dollar* <u>*Challenge*</u>
with *The Big Payoff*,
Tic-Tac-Dough,
Name That Tune
Top Dollar —
just saying the names
it's like *Open Sesame* —
Quiz Kids
Down You Go

The Big Surprise
Strike It Rich
and my masterpiece
Twenty-One
Television:
the perfect machine
for this moment
when society
is so nearly a perfect machine
that the only chore left for us
is to make it make our happiness!
But listen:
I see darkness ahead,
darkness and despair;
we're past the days —
and they were good days, make no mistake —
Days when a test pattern
would mesmerize the nation.
People are ingrates, sad to say,
ingrates to technology
as they're ingrates to God.
And can we blame the people, can we?
When week after week
on our little show
it might as well be the butcher
carrying off the prize,
might as well be neurasthenic auntie
or cousin Homer with the problem —
Might as well?
Hell, it is!
The time has come,
we need a Hero.
We need the tall man,
the tall, graceful, brilliant, virile
and undeflectably *deserving* man —
We need a hero
and I'll make a hero
and I'll make him *now*

because, cliché:
There's no time like the present
and no time to waste.
Good evening.
(Lights. Title: At Night Across America, People Watch ... Twenty-One scene illuminated: Two Contestants/Jack Barry; watching on TV the Twenty-One scene: Enright, Freedman, Sponsor (Ben), and Network Guy (Roger). On Twenty-One, the Contestant is stumped. Long silence.)
SPONSOR.
This is pathetic.
FREEDMAN.
It'll get better.
SPONSOR.
Dan, what am I watching?
ENRIGHT.
Intense concentration.
This is suspense, Ben.
SPONSOR.
Uh-huh.
(Pause.)
I like silence.
Silence is good.
I'm a fan of silence.
In its place.
Church.
You know — when you're praying?
ENRIGHT.
Sure.
SPONSOR.
But in front of how many million TV viewers?
Though by now it's probably five sleepy drunks —
Roger, tell me, is this really
the sort of behavior the network likes to see on its shows?
NETWORK.
We think *Twenty-One* has enormous potential, Ben.
I was just saying the other —
wait! — look! —

There's going to be talking!
BARRY.
I'm sorry — your time is up —
SPONSOR.
Oh, for crying out loud!
BARRY.
The answer is Austria, Sweden, Russia and —
(Sponsor turns TV off — fade Twenty-One.*)*
ENRIGHT.
Granted, we've had better weeks —
SPONSOR.
This has been a streak.
FREEDMAN.
Toss of the dice.
Hah-hah.
SPONSOR.
Are these the Einsteins you promised me?
These people who sit in the isolation booth
and file their nails for thirty seconds
while they try to remember what the nuns taught them
and *fail?*
Dan, I have a product to push,
I have to appeal to geriatrics.
I watch this
(Turns on set. We see another stumped Contestant.)
— louder, pumpkin —
I watch this and I think:
My eighty-year-old ladies are not going to be loving —
I mean, *this?*
The stammering
the blank stares
At best, it will remind them that they're senile.
Is that a jolly evening by the hearth?
ENRIGHT.
Look, Ben,
the talent we recruit
is the talent we recruit,
there's no predicti —

SPONSOR.
So are you saying
I'm going to spend my whole season
watching dummies say nothing
or is something better coming along?
(Beat.)
FREEDMAN.
Well ...
NETWORK.
It's a game of *chance*, Ben
— nobody knows everything —
In games of chance,
sometimes the gods are *with* you,
sometimes the gods are *without* you —
ENRIGHT.
Actually, there is someone.
SPONSOR.
Yes?
ENRIGHT.
A guy who came in,
took the test recently,
scored higher than anybody ever has ...
SPONSOR.
So?
ENRIGHT.
He's not really at all what I had in mind,
but he's almost certain to be a champion.
Trouble is
he's ...
peculiar, a little.
SPONSOR.
That's all I need.
ENRIGHT.
But only by nature!
He's ... vivid ...
Goes to City College.
Was in the Army.

G.I. Joe with stage presence
(of a sort).
His name is Herb Stempel.
He might be
you know, he might be
he's the old idea
but I think there's some blood left in that stone,
if he wins.
(Beat.)
SPONSOR.
Good.
Because Loretta Young's looking for new sponsorship, you know.
I got Loretta Young breathing down my neck.
ENRIGHT.
Why, Ben,
some people would find that downright erotic.
SPONSOR.
Ahh — she's a goddamn prude.
You've gotta pay her a fine
every time you use a swear word.
FREEDMAN.
Fuck that.
SPONSOR.
So ... next week?
ENRIGHT.
Next week.
NETWORK.   *(Exiting with Sponsor.)*
Come on, Ben,
let me buy you a —
oh, you've given it up, haven't you?
(Enright and Freedman are left alone. Freedman watches after them to make sure they're really gone.)
FREEDMAN.
So, does this, at least, cause you concern?
ENRIGHT.
Do you know my theory,
Al, do you know my theory
of what links certain people?

FREEDMAN.
No, Dan.
ENRIGHT.
There is a fuse, Al, I think,
a kind of fuse
that links the unlikeliest people.
It leaps over the most profound, the most amazing chasms,
chasms of class
of race and intellect and religion
and good and evil
and joins, uh, say,
Hitler and *Gandhi* —
Marilyn Monroe and Douglas MacArthur,
Patti Page and *Buddha* —
FREEDMAN.
The point of this bullshit being ...
ENRIGHT.
The point of this bullshit being
Twenty-One is not going down the toilet —
it's not my destiny.
I've been thinking ...
FREEDMAN.
... Now?
ENRIGHT.
Yes, now, I think.
(Lights.)
Whose idea was it?
FREEDMAN.
Who remembers?
ENRIGHT. *(To us through this section.)*
The contestants have to have charisma —
FREEDMAN.
— to attract the viewers —
ENRIGHT.
They have to have brains —
FREEDMAN.
— to be persuasive in interviews —

ENRIGHT.
They have to keep secrets well —
FREEDMAN.
— To save our asses.
ENRIGHT.
Provide a star next week.
Preparations must get underway immediately.
I call Mr. Stempel.
FREEDMAN.
His wife is at the movies.
He's home baby-sitting.
ENRIGHT.
I get myself to Forest Hills.
It begins.
(Enright is in Stempel's home. Reading from cards.)
This unfinished church
is one of the landmarks of Barcelona, Spain —
STEMPEL.
Say no more —
I've got it, I've got it:
The Church of the Holy Family
actually commenced by Francesco del Vilar in 1882,
but taken over by the famed genius Antonio Gaudi
the following year and continued by him
until 1926 when he was run over by a Barcelona streetcar.
And killed.
Needless to say.
So he stopped.
Shall I describe its lineaments?
Thirteen tubular towers were planned,
pillars that swayed,
very peculiar —
ENRIGHT.
No, no, no —
not necessary.
You've answered the question.
STEMPEL.
After his death,

his friends and assistants —
ENRIGHT.
Herb —
STEMPEL.
— continued to work to finish —
ENRIGHT.
Herb.
Done.
STEMPEL.
Oh, oh, sure.
(Beat.)
Because only one of the tubes and one transept were completed when he —
ENRIGHT.
Moving on —
STEMPEL.
— kicked it.
Gotcha.
Go.
ENRIGHT.
What is the capital of Nepal?
STEMPEL.
Oh, please.
ENRIGHT.
We don't pay for "oh, please."
STEMPEL.
Katmandu.
ENRIGHT.
Very good.
STEMPEL.
The official language is Nepali,
a derivative of Sanskrit.
Other major cities are Bakhtapur and Lalitpur.
Would you like to know about irrigation?
ENRIGHT.
No.
STEMPEL.
Because it's *lousy.*

I can't help it —
I know these things!
I'm bursting!
ENRIGHT.
Great.
I love your enthusiasm —
Now —
The category is —
STEMPEL.
Uh,
Mr. Enright,
before we proceed further
may I ask you a question
somewhat off the beaten path?
ENRIGHT.
Certainly.
STEMPEL.
Do you think that this exposure
will abet me in the furtherance of my career?
ENRIGHT.
What career is that?
STEMPEL.
Didn't you read my information card?
ENRIGHT.
I'm sure I did.
I'm sorry, I must have forgotten —
STEMPEL.
My *acting* career!
I'm going to be an actor ...
Why are you looking at me that way?
ENRIGHT.
Something in my eye.
(Rubs his eye.)
STEMPEL.
I've wanted to be an actor since high school —
ENRIGHT.
I'm sure you're

... a very good —
so —
STEMPEL.
I'm told I show enormous *potential*
despite an unfortunate propensity towards being *miscast* —
ENRIGHT.
That's a nice story;
okay, the cate —
STEMPEL.
But it seems to me
that now is my perfect moment
what with this new vogue
for kitchen sink realism, you know:
Ernie Borgnine
Rod Steiger
Playhouse 90 and so forth
I think I'm a very realistic type, don't you?
ENRIGHT.
Absolutely.
STEMPEL.
So do you think
my exposure on *Twenty-One*
will *aid* my acting chances?
Answer, already.
(Beat.)
ENRIGHT.
I can say this:
It certainly won't *lessen* your chances.
STEMPEL.
... Good.
That's fine,
very fair,
sorry to importune,
go on ...
ENRIGHT.
The category is National Anthems.
STEMPEL.
Wonderful —

I'm an expert
because —
ENRIGHT.
Give me the name
and the first line
of the national anthem of South Africa.
STEMPEL.
South Africa.
Okay.
The name and the first line of the national anthem
of South Africa are ...
South.
Africa.
Because, of course, *Sweden* is
Du gamla, du fria
and it goes
"Du gamla, du fria
du fjalhoga nord:"
Or: "Thou ancient, thou freeborn,
thou mountainous North."
ENRIGHT.
South Africa.
STEMPEL.
I'm getting there, I'm getting there!
South Africa, it's ...
Huh.
This is so unusual.
There seems to be a disturbance in my brainpan
I ...
ENRIGHT.
It's —
STEMPEL.
No, no, no, give me a second!
It's ...
Um ...
ENRIGHT.
Well, of course,

it's *Die stem van Suid-Afrika,*
isn't it?
STEMPEL.
Of course!
Of course it is!
(Strikes forehead with palm.)
Idiot!
Jerk!
Dum-dum!
"*Die stem van Suid-Afrika* ... "
"*Die stem van Suid-Afrika.*"
ENRIGHT.
Which means ...
STEMPEL.
The ... uh ...
The song —
ENRIGHT.
The *call* —
STEMPEL.
The *call* —
that's what I meant —
of South Africa.
ENRIGHT.
And the first line is,
"*Uit die bloue van onse hemel
uit die diepte van ons see* ... "
STEMPEL.
"*Uit die bloue van onse hemel
uit die diepte van ons see.*"
ENRIGHT.
Which, of course, means
"Ringing out from our blue heavens;
from our deep seas breaking round."
STEMPEL.
"Ringing out from our blue heavens;
from our deep seas breaking round."
I *knew* that —

I must have had a little stroke —
a *petit-mal,* or whatever.
ENRIGHT.
I don't doubt you, Herb.
STEMPEL.
So, can I ask you something?
ENRIGHT.
Sure, sure.
STEMPEL.
The real questions —
are they gonna be like these?
ENRIGHT.
Well.
STEMPEL.
You don't have to —
If that's giving something away or —
ENRIGHT.
No.
No.
Will the real questions be like these?
That's a real *poser,* isn't it?
STEMPEL.
It is?
ENRIGHT.
Because, I mean,
we do sometimes say, don't we?
that a person is behaving in a way that's so *like* himself?
Don't we?
Or so *unlike* himself?
STEMPEL.
... Uh ... yes ...
ENRIGHT.
So, I suppose by that logic, yes —
These questions are very "like" the real ones.
STEMPEL.
Oh ...
Oh!

ENRIGHT.
Memorize this:
You'll begin by asking for a nine point question.
You'll answer that correctly.
You'll stutter a little as you do.
We'll turn off the air in the isolation booth
to make you sweat.
You'll follow that question with another nine point question.
Another correct answer.
Stuttering.
Sweating.
Then —
STEMPEL.
Excuse me — !
Is this really how it works?
ENRIGHT.
Yes.
This is how it works.
STEMPEL.
Because I thought
the points and all —
I thought that was my choice.
ENRIGHT.
It is.
Of course it is.
You'll *choose* a nine point question.
Then you'll *choose* another.
Those will be your choices.
What's the problem?
STEMPEL.
... No.
Nothing ...
No ...
ENRIGHT.
Of course
you'll mention this to no one.
(*Beat. They look at each other.*)
'Cause, you know, this could cause

me a whole lot of *tsuris*.
But when we met
I had this instinct ...
I mean, I *think* I know I can trust you.
(Beat. Stempel smiles tentatively.)
Where's your closet?
We need to dress you for the show.
STEMPEL.
Uh-huh.
Yes.
Actually
I figured what I'm wearing now
was
was
was
with of course the jacket that goes with
and a regimental tie
I thought —
ENRIGHT.
No.
STEMPEL.
Jeez.
So, this isn't good huh?
Funny
because what I'm wearing is actually from Brooks Brothers
the noted haberdashery?
ENRIGHT.
Mm-hm.
STEMPEL.
Not that I think
that's any *guarantee* —
I'm no patsy to a reputation
I know even the finest of emporia
can
can
can
commit a *gaffe*.

ENRIGHT.   *(Offers a shiny suit.)*
Try this.
STEMPEL.
— and, of course, sometimes even the right clothes
don't work on the wrong man —
I've got a problematic frame,
but I thought
I thought ...
This?
This you want me to try?
ENRIGHT.
Yes, try this.
STEMPEL.
This is actually not —
This is my *father*-in-law's
truth be known
A nice —
a prosperous man
but *prust*
if you know what I mean.
His taste is very Pitkin Avenue
so I ... uh ...
I, uh ...
ENRIGHT.
Just try it.
STEMPEL.
This?
Really?
Because I'd hoped to make a nice impression —
ENRIGHT.
I think this *will* make a nice impression —
STEMPEL.   *(Shrugs, begins to undress.)*
Okay.
You're the expert.
Um ... you know, what happened before
— the South Africa thing —
that was a very unusual —
a very one-in-a-million type thing.

Usually, I'm not of the mistake-makers.
These clothes
My father-in-law
he's a smaller man than myself —
ENRIGHT.
That's all right —
STEMPEL.
As I was saying:
Normally, you ask a question
and I'm not stumped.
"Not-stumped Herb," they call me
— well, not really —
You see, I've got what they call
an "eidetic" memory —
did you ever hear of that?
It's like a photographic memory
only I prefer the word "eidetic"
because fewer people know it —
How does this look?
'Cause it feels like shit.
ENRIGHT.
It's perfect.
STEMPEL.
Could my taste be superior to yours, Mr. Enright?
A joke.
ENRIGHT.
You're a serviceman —
STEMPEL.
Ex — thank you very much.
ENRIGHT.
You go to City College nights —
STEMPEL.
Sometimes days —
ENRIGHT.
You're from Brooklyn —
STEMPEL.
Mr. Enright,
no offense,

but this is *Queens*.
ENRIGHT.
... You have some *past* with Brooklyn, though, don't —
STEMPEL.
Everyone has some past with Brooklyn but —
ENRIGHT.
Brooklyn is better.
You're married.
STEMPEL.
My wife, Toby, is a very beautiful woman
... what are you looking?
ENRIGHT.
You have a child —
STEMPEL.
— my baby, my boy —
ENRIGHT.
You're poor —
STEMPEL.
My in-laws are quite comfortable;
they help us out —
a wonderful family
full of terrible people;
except my wi —
ENRIGHT.
Give me your watch.
STEMPEL.
— My —
ENRIGHT.
I hear something.
... I promise I'll return it.
(Stempel hands it over.)
There.
You trust me.
(He puts it up to his ear.)
That's what I thought —
the ticking is extraordinarily loud.
STEMPEL.
I don't have to wear it —

it's only a talisman —
ENRIGHT.
No, Herb, you *will* wear it —
Close to the microphone.
Sweating
Stuttering
Ticking
Poor;
Can this man put bread on the table?
Will his child perish
of some poor-person's disease
in terrible Brooklyn?
Tune in next week.
Hypnotic.
Splendid.
We'll all make a lot of money ...
(Pause.)
STEMPEL.   *(Suddenly, almost in a rage.)*
Look —
I just want you to know —
If this isn't how it's done —
If I'm a special case —
You know, "Good for the Jews" or something —
I don't need it —
I'm a fantastic answerer —
I know all the answers —
I can do it myself!
I can do it myself.
These clothes.... Jeez.
My wife thinks I'm attractive.
ENRIGHT.
This *is* how it's done —
I can assure you.
Herb — really — you're about to be a champion.
STEMPEL.
... Yes.
Very true.
In that case, I'm happy to oblige.

(Toby enters.)
TOBY.
Herb — ? Is the baby — ?
(Sees Enright.)
Oh.
Who's — ?
STEMPEL.
Toby, this is Mr. Enright.
I'll tell you in a minute.
ENRIGHT. *(Extending hand.)*
Mrs. Stempel —
it's nice to meet you.
I'd best be going.
Herb —
we'll be talking over the next few days.
STEMPEL.
Yes. Yes.
Thank you. Thank you so much.
(Enright exits.)
TOBY.
Who is he?
STEMPEL.
Good news.
TOBY.
Why are you wearing that terrible suit?
(Lights. Tight: From the Pages of The Christian Century. *Editorialists appear as they speak.)*
EDITORIALIST.
Television,
that circle of Hell
Dante himself could not imagine,
is, with these "quiz programs,"
subjecting the American people
to the most blatant and sustained attempt
to aggravate covetous instincts
that has ever been turned against an entire population.
Television,
that foul black pit

is now about the task of inundating the nation
with an orgy of gambling
and turning the multitudes who submit
into a money-bedazzled mob,
a scurrying swarm of greed-crazed maggots
pantingly hopeful that here at last
they will find the magic
that will lead them to the pot of gold at the rainbow's end.
(Lights. Title: Mr. Stempel Makes His Debut. Projection: Stempel's face — faintly. As scene starts, it's played out on Twenty-One *set with acoustic sound. Gradually, projection becomes more vivid, acoustic sound is doubled by recorded sound, the live action fades to silhouette and acoustic sound stops.)*
BARRY.
... And our next contestant is former G.I. Herbert Stempel,
a native of Brooklyn, New York.
How is Brooklyn these days, Herb?
STEMPEL.
Oh, it's a very lovely borough, Mr. Barry.
BARRY.
And is that tree still growing there?
STEMPEL.
Oh, ha-ha,
yes indeed, Mr. Barry,
it certainly is.
BARRY.
All right, Herb,
let's play the game.
(As Stempel crosses into booth and puts on headphones.)
The category is National Anthems.
How many points would you like?
(Projection: Stempel — close-up.)
STEMPEL.
Golly,
National Anthems, is it?
Well, I think I know a fair amount about them —
I'm going to try nine points.

BARRY.
Nine points for your first question!
I'm sure all your friends at C.C.N.Y. College
are as impressed by your courage
as we are here.
STEMPEL.
I hope so, Mr. Barry.
BARRY.
Here's your question,
let's see how you do:
Give me the name
and the first line
of the national anthem for South Africa.
STEMPEL.
South Africa....
Jeepers, that's a hard one ...
BARRY.
You have a little time ...
(Projection: Stempel's face, obviously sweating. Projection: Stempel head-to-torso, the bunching of his jacket around his midriff.)
STEMPEL.
Let me see ...
(The loud ticking of a watch. Projection: Stempel mopping his damp brow — the cuffs of his shirt are frayed.)
Wou — would that be,
"*Die Stem* ...
Die Stem fon — no <u>van</u> —
Die Stem van Suid-Afrika"
and does it go
"*Uit die bloue van onse hemel
uit die diepte ... von ... ons ... see?*
The Call of South Africa:
"Ringing out from our blue heavens
from our deep seas breaking round ..."?
BARRY.
Well, Herb, Stempel,
I can see you're going to be a Big Dog on Campus tomorrow
if you keep playing like that ...

(Projection: Stempel smiling. Lights. A housewife appears.)
HOUSEWIFE.
To the producers, director, inventors, creators and star of the *Twenty-One* program and to the folks that brought us Geritol,
Dear Sirs:
This has been a difficult time
for my husband and me.
My husband has recently been promoted to
a new job that causes him
greater-than-desirable anxiety.
Two weeks ago
a fire started in our barbecue pit
and our fallout shelter melted.
(Fade in. Sponsor's office. Sponsor and Enright: Sponsor reading letter.)
SPONSOR and HOUSEWIFE.
I like to relax with your show.
But your new champion makes me nervous.
He *reminds* me of something.
He makes me want to take a *shower.*
He makes me scratch myself —
(Fade on Housewife.)
ENRIGHT.
She sounds totally crackers, Ben —
SPONSOR. *(Flurrying many pages at him.)*
Dan — they can't all be crackers!
ENRIGHT.
Don't be too sure of that —
SPONSOR. *(Overlaps.)*
I need something I can look at,
something to enjoy — like my ottoman —
ENRIGHT.
I beg your —
SPONSOR. *(Continuous.)*
I never think about my ottoman
but I'm always glad it's there,
week after week after week after

ENRIGHT. *(Overlaps.)*
I understand, believe me, I'm searching,
but in the meantime, you have to understand,
this is what's happening:
"The fascination of the abomination."
SPONSOR.
Christ, it was a dark day when you went to college.
What the hell does that —
ENRIGHT. *(Overlaps.)*
You see
You hate
You can't look away
and then something better comes along —
Think of traffic accidents,
no — think of tooth pain —
SPONSOR.
What?
ENRIGHT.
How wonderful it feels when it's over.
(Enright/Sponsor exit. Lights up on: Stempel's. Toby bundled in front of TV.)
STEMPEL.
Sweetheart — ?
Honey — ?
Are you sleeping?
TOBY.
No.
I don't sleep.
Don't wake the baby —
STEMPEL. *(Overlapped.)*
The baby's sleeping.
TOBY.
Okay ...
What did you do tonight?
STEMPEL.
Oh, it was a very, very beautiful night.
You should have met me.

Why didn't you meet — ?
TOBY.
The baby —
STEMPEL.
You know you could have gotten
your mother to sit with the baby;
she *loves* to do —
TOBY.
I couldn't
anyway I didn't
anyway so what
so what did you do?
STEMPEL.
After class,
I got together with Hal and Nat
we had an early dinner in the Village
this I-tie place —
TOBY.
Who are Hal and Nat?
STEMPEL.
They're new, they're since the show, they're ...
So after dinner
we take this walk
forty blocks —
TOBY.
— without a coat?
STEMPEL.
I was *fine*.
We go to Town Hall
and listen to the Modern Jazz Quartet.
When they play, "Themes from 'No Sun in Venice'"
I swear to you
I'm in a canal,
everywhere I look:
doges
really —
a transporting —

TOBY.
— that's nice —
STEMPEL.   *(Overlapped.)*
— thing,
yeah, it was so nice.
It was so nice.
And after
it turns out Nat
knows John Lewis —
TOBY.
Who's John Lewis?
STEMPEL.
The head of the MJQ!
Negro fella —
So we go back
he introduces me
my palms are sweating
'cause this is such an *event*
this man is a *genius*
And he says
Nat says
"John Lewis, I'd like you to meet —"
And before he can *finish*
Lewis says to me,
"You're Herb Stempel, aren't you?"
And I said,
"In fact I am ..."
(Beat.)
It seemed like a bigger story
when it was happening
but it was ... it was ...
TOBY.
That must have been very —
STEMPEL.
It was
yeah, it was
... So are you sleepy?
Why can't you sleep?

TOBY.
You know, I get that way.
(Beat. He looks at her tenderly.)
STEMPEL.
You look so pretty.
TOBY.
Oh, sure ...
STEMPEL.
You *do* ...
TOBY.
I'm a little tense lately.
STEMPEL.
About what?
Why would you be tense?
TOBY.
Nothing.
People.
Whatever.
They chit-chat —
blah-blah-blah
this and that.
STEMPEL.
No they *don't!*
Things are not like that.
Why do you
Things are actually very —
TOBY.
Don't say it —
STEMPEL.
But they're —
TOBY.
Don't give it a *kinahurra* —
STEMPEL.
All right.
(Beat.)
So, anyway,
you know, I told Mr. Enright
about our financial situation

and he gave me an advance —
TOBY.
An advance on what?
STEMPEL.
An advance on my winnings.
TOBY.
What if you don't win?
STEMPEL.
... He has *faith!*
Anyway, it's rather sizable
so I was thinking
maybe I could get you a present ...
TOBY.
We've got *bills* to pay —
STEMPEL.
But something *nice*
A *luxury* ...
TOBY.
Like what?
STEMPEL.
How would you like a little analysis?
(Beat.)
TOBY.
Do you think I'm not normal?
STEMPEL.
That has nothing to do with it — !
TOBY.
I get a little nervous sometimes —
There are things to be nervous about,
why shouldn't I —
STEMPEL.
Look, that's such a
a *misconception* about what analysis —
it's about *knowledge.*
Knowledge is a wonderful thing.
Knowledge will make you free.
The finest minds of your time —
at *Dissent* magazine they don't

even give you a job interview
unless you've had five years with a qualified Freudian.
(He laughs.)
TOBY.
I don't want to — my father offered that time and I —
STEMPEL.
I can pay for my own wife's analysis, thank you very much!
TOBY.
Anyway, it's not me; it's you;
every good comes thirteen-to-the-dozen bad with you.
The minute things turn around
you know how you get
all crazy, all whatever;
why shouldn't I be a little
STEMPEL.   *(Overlaps from "the minute.")*
Me?
I'm not the one who's terminally morose!
I'm not the one who's photo-phobic!
I'm not —
STOP!
(They stop.)
No, I mean ...
If I hold you,
do you think maybe you'll fall asleep?
TOBY.
I don't know.
Maybe.
(He sits beside her, holds her.)
STEMPEL.
It was such a wonderful concert ...
I wish you were there.
I swear you would have seen Venice.
TOBY.
Mmm ...
STEMPEL.
I'd hum it for you
because I remember every bar,
except it's jazz

and too much happens in it ...
(Charles solo.)
CHARLES.
I'm sorry I'm so late —
I was way the way uptown
— well, Morningside Heights —
and I was teaching this background sort of history
for my freshman America lit class
and we got into this very earnest, terribly probing,
basically vacant
theological dispute
and, well,
Talmudic scholars concede a point
faster than an eighteen-year-old
at an Ivy League college
so I had to clear that up
— which I'm by no means certain I did —
and that meant I was running late,
then that sudden rainstorm
and I couldn't find my umbrella,
then the subway broke down,
I had the wrong address,
and did you know your elevators
were stalled for twenty minutes?
But here I am
tardy, apologetic, and, uh, somewhat damp,
I'm afraid.
(Lights. Enright's office.)
ENRIGHT.
Mr. Van Doren — it's good to meet you!
CHARLES.
I hope you'll forgive me —
ENRIGHT.
Oh, of course — I've been waiting months for this — another half-hour doesn't —
CHARLES.
I beg your —

ENRIGHT.
Nothing. I would have met you at Columbia if you'd —
CHARLES.
No. I wanted to see what all this looks like.
ENRIGHT.
Oh. Good.
(Doris takes Charles' coat.)
CHARLES.
Thank you.
ENRIGHT.
Have a seat, Mr. Van ... Charles, may I?
CHARLES.
Yes, sure.
ENRIGHT.
Charlie; then
CHARLES.
Charles, I think ... would probably —
ENRIGHT.
Charles,
what was that theological dispute about,
if you don't mind my —
CHARLES.
Oh God —
I was trying to explain to them
the idea of grace.
ENRIGHT.
I see —
and they couldn't follow the idea of grace?
CHARLES.
No, they could follow it well enough
but they seemed to resent its implications.
You see,
I kept insisting that
what defines grace is
it's God's will and has nothing to do with how people act;
and *they* kept insisting
that means you can behave like a jerk and still be saved,
and that offends them as, I don't know, A*me*ricans or someth —

39

ENRIGHT.
I can see you love to teach, Charles.
CHARLES.
It's all right.
Well ... you know ...
"Youth."
ENRIGHT.
You don't care for "Youth?"
CHARLES.
They're fine.
It's just
I'm too old to *be* Youth
and too young to *crave* it
which means I'm mostly irritated by it
when it comes to me *en masse*, at least,
as it does every single
... I love to teach, yes.
This office doesn't look anything like what I'd expected.
ENRIGHT.
What did you —
CHARLES.
Oh, I don't know, really.
Dancing girls? Or *ponies*.
Something ... less subdued.
ENRIGHT.
And instead, it all looks distressingly
like your own office at Columbia —
CHARLES.
No, now,
Columbia is coated in this kind of nineteenth-century *soot*,
this doesn't look like Columbia, but —
ENRIGHT.
But already we're shattering your misconceptions about
television —
CHARLES.
I don't really have any strong misconceptions.
I mean, I haven't particularly *dwelled* on it.
I don't even own a television set, to tell the —

ENRIGHT.
We'll fix that
once you appear on our show.
CHARLES.
I —
ENRIGHT.
We *want* you on the show, Charles.
We want you to start next week.
CHARLES.
… Yes.
Damn.
That's the thing, you see.
My *guess* is that … I can't actually do this at all.
(Beat.)
ENRIGHT.
Then why are you here?
CHARLES.
Yes. Well, I thought I should explain.
You see, I was in this bar with a friend
and your show was on their television
and I more-or-less fell into answering the questions.
And it seemed I got rather a high percentage right,
so —
ENRIGHT.
Yours was among the highest grades every registered on our test,
just by the way —
CHARLES.
Is that so?
Well, that's very nice to —
among the highest?
ENRIGHT.
Perhaps the very highest.
I can check if you like —
CHARLES.
No.
No, no, no,
of course not.

Listen, I know there's something absurd about my
dithering this way —
after all, it's not a life-and-death decision —
ENRIGHT.
Then why are your shoulders so tense?
CHARLES.
My
I beg your pardon?
ENRIGHT.
Am I making you nervous
or are you just a chronic brooder or
CHARLES.
Not
really, no, in my family
I'm considered the happy-go-lucky one.
Of course, that may just mean the dummy.
ENRIGHT.
Dummy!
You, Charles?
That's
(Consults cards.)
Doctorate in Mathematics (almost)
A year at the Sorbonne (well, a summer)
Astronomy major for a good little while
Doctorate in literature (before you know it)
Clarinet (almost concert level)
For pity's sake, Charles,
you're a Renaissance Man!
CHARLES. *(Almost muttering, almost to himself.)*
Must have been ... some other Renaissance.
ENRIGHT. *(Overlaps.)*
I know who you are, by the way.
I should admit this.
CHARLES.
Do you?
ENRIGHT.
By which I mean,
I know who your *father* is.

CHARLES.
... Ah.
Everybody does.
ENRIGHT.
Well, I mean, sure
(Consults cards.)
Pulitzer for Poetry;
Author of the definitive biography of Hawthorne —
CHARLES.
These *cards* of yours —
ENRIGHT.
Eminent critic,
eminent short story writer;
Pre-eminent teacher
when *he* was at Columbia,
the teacher of, who, Lionel Trilling
(Reading:)
Thomas Merton, Allan Ginsberg (really?), Whittaker
Chambers (this list is peculiar) —
CHARLES.
Yes, I'm familiar with the roll — !
ENRIGHT.
... This upsets you.
CHARLES.
Not at all.
ENRIGHT.
Beloved in the classroom
but a cold fish at home?
CHARLES.
Exceptionally warm, in fact.
As monuments go.
No. Very warm.
ENRIGHT.
Yes.
Anyway
I know who your father is.
And your mother and your uncle and your aunt
— very Gilbert and Sullivan, isn't it? —

What I mean is
I know what made you
I can imagine what restrains you.
But why let it?
Why not
go on TV
make a bundle
and then take a sabbatical
and
I don't know
write your *novel* or someth —
CHARLES.
In the first place
I've already written my novel
and it's not an experience I much care to repeat,
but beyond that,
I have certain —
ENRIGHT. *(Overlaps.)*
And what was it about?
CHARLES.
What … was…?
ENRIGHT.
The *novel.*
CHARLES.
Oh … the novel …
ENRIGHT.
Yes, — what was it about?
CHARLES.
Patricide.
(Beat.)
Right, I know:
"Oh, please"
but no, you see
I've always been interested in classical ideas and —
ENRIGHT.
Did your father like it?
CHARLES.
Very much.

He always likes everything I do — it's a sort of mania in him —
but my *point* is
I'm a teacher now.
And that's a tricky sort of business
and terribly old-fashioned so
I
can't be on a quiz show, I'm afraid.
ENRIGHT.
... Huh!
CHARLES.
... I just don't think I can probably do it.
ENRIGHT.
... I'm wondering —
CHARLES.
What?
ENRIGHT.
The obvious frustration you feel —
is it *because* you're so young
and what you do is so nearly archaic?
CHARLES.
... I'm *sorry?*
ENRIGHT.
Well, you just said so yourself —
CHARLES.
I did? When was that?
ENRIGHT.
And in a way
I guess I have to agree with you
because
well
who are the Van Dorens
really
these days?
This somewhat fading tradition in American letters,
yes?
Holdovers from the nineteenth
the *best* of the nineteenth century —
I remember reading your father in college

and it was lovely
but I always pictured him on a hilltop somewhere,
chatting with the Oversoul,
experiencing Immediate Truth —
CHARLES. *(Overlapped.)*
You're supposed to be wooing me;
decimating my forebears is a pretty odd way to go about it —
ENRIGHT. *(Overlaps.)*
I overstepped.
Forgive me.
CHARLES.
No, that's fine, it's just you're so ... depressingly *on-target*.
ENRIGHT.
I'm sorry;
I didn't mean to be.
CHARLES.
... We are a little bit ... waning ... this family.
And I've just started.
It's a peculiar feeling
giving yourself to something
you're bound to outlast
but it's what I've learned so —
You know, we should have met at Columbia —
I wouldn't have told you this there.
ENRIGHT.
But isn't this where I come in?
(Charles looks at him.)
Listen, Charlie,
you don't own a television now;
that was a very cute remark — you will.
Sooner or later everybo — *all* of us
will be watching, watching
the same things, watch —
*sha*ring an unprecedented amount of *something*.
What will it be?
Will it lift us
or will it lower us?
This is

look, this is my secret strategy
— don't tell, it's, no one knows —
I am taking
this lowliest thing
this quiz show *thing*
and pouring into it everything I value
that I don't want to see go out of the world.
Which is why I need you.
CHARLES.
... I don't see —
ENRIGHT.
With that retiring egghead quality you have
your superior misfitedness.
That shy, "every-mother's-daughter-should-marry-it" sort of —
sex appeal.
CHARLES.   (*Overlaps.*)
I think this is making me uncomfortable.
ENRIGHT.
but you're not *sure*....
Think of it, Charles:
There you'll be
winning
(I'm sure of it.)
thousands upon thousands upon thousands of dol —
what do Columbia instructors *make,* by the way,
don't answer —
And out there, Mr. and Mrs. America
they get all hot and bothered by your triumph,
they start steaming over the World Book *Encyclopedia* or
    someth —
proud to learn the, you know,
population of Bolivia and its primary crops.
Because of you, Charles:
Off with the TV,
on with the mind!
Use the medium to subvert the medium.
Isn't that kind of irony —
I mean, I'm sorry,

but wouldn't you call it,
literary?
CHARLES.
Mr. Enright,
were you trained by Jesuits?
ENRIGHT.
You're mocking me.
CHARLES.
God, no.
In fact you've very nearly *won.*
Except ...
I have the most tremendous gaps.
I might be able to explain some obscure aspect
of quantum theory
then you could say to me,
"What's that flower?"
and I'd be lost —
ENRIGHT.
The point of this being —
CHARLES.
... What if I don't win?
ENRIGHT.   *(Rising and extending hand.)*
Shall we discuss that in a couple of days?
(Lights. Rabid fan appears. Stempel in projection and silhouette in booth.)
TOBY.
Herb?
Are you sleeping?
So sleep,
but listen:
I had Mr. Dolman over this afternoon for tea.
You know: Terry? That new man from upstairs?
I thought it was neighborly
and Terry — he's been watching you
he *admires* you
and you know what he was saying?
He was saying we could *use* the money, you know?
And we don't. We *spend* it, but we don't *use* it — a distinction.

And here's how, he said:
Something about Florida and horses and investing —
he must be an expert — I didn't understand a word
but when he said Florida, I thought:
(Lights on Charles.)
CHARLES.
Dad:
I wonder
have you ever heard about these quiz show things?
Because the other day I sort of ran into one
and it seems they want me.
It seems they think my presence might be important.
Well of course it's not important
it's a lark but
I tell you, they showed me around and
it's the most peculiar world.
TOBY.
It's not just where the *alte kakes* go to lay down —
it's for young people too and us —
CHARLES.
It's filled with wonderfully intelligent people
who are also somehow mindless
— and there's color and money and action —
and some kind of high purpose
buried in there, too —
TOBY.
and I know you think I don't like anything and I'm sorry
and besides it's not true, I like *many* things
just not anything I ever have
but Herb —
CHARLES.
It doesn't suit me at all,
which may make it just the thing for now.
What I mean is —
TOBY.
I mean, I don't like it here
CHARLES.
It's not that they don't know who we are

TOBY.
because people know us here
CHARLES.
but somehow they made me feel terrifically *unrecognized.*
TOBY.
and when he said Florida
CHARLES.
I mean, television — my God — !
TOBY.
I thought,
Well, this is somewhere else
CHARLES.
It's like when you started reviewing movies
back at the beginning of talkies
and everyone said, why bother,
but you ventured in and found
TOBY
someplace we've never been before.
CHARLES.
No — what I mean is,
it might be fun ...
and you've said yourself
I've been a little short on fun lately.
And I think you're right.
Short on ... everything —
TOBY. *(On "everything.")*
And I must have looked interested because Mr. Dolman said
    to me, "calm down."
CHARLES.
I know you'll approve of this
but would you do me a favor?
TOBY.
So could we think about this maybe?
CHARLES.
Would you consider approving
a little less quickly this time?
TOBY.
Please?

CHARLES.
All my love,
Charlie.
TOBY.
Herb?
(Lights.)
STEMPEL. *(Voice over and booth.)*
And the name of that play is:
RABID FAN.
This guy on your show:
STEMPEL.
Life is a Dream
RABID FAN.
I HATE HIM LIKE RABIES!
(Lights. Enright and Charles. Enright leans against desk with cards. Charles stands, paces. Two days later.)
CHARLES.
The four Balearic Islands are ...
ENRIGHT.
You have a little time ...
CHARLES.
Majorca, Minorca ... Ibiza and ...
I don't remember — *For* — something
For*mo*sa ... For*mi*ca ... For-men-on-a-horse
I don't know
ENRIGHT.
Formentera
CHARLES.
Formentera!
ENRIGHT.
Once again.
CHARLES.
Majorca, Minorca, Ibiza, and Formentera.
ENRIGHT.
Very good.
Now.
The four Balearic Islands are ...

CHARLES.
... Majorca, Min —
is my voice too high or too fast or someth —
ENRIGHT.
It's fine.
CHARLES.
Is my posture bad or —
ENRIGHT.
You're entirely excellent.
The four Balearic Islands are
CHARLES.
... Majorca —
do you have some private obsession with this region of the
    world —
ENRIGHT.
Not at all.
CHARLES.
Then why do we keep hammering away at this?
ENRIGHT.
I think repetition is good
CHARLES. *(Over; complaining but pleasantly.)*
Or why do we keep on with this at all
if I'm coming off all right?
I mean, you said this was for
elocution or something,
and if that's okay, why do we —
ENRIGHT.
I think that —
CHARLES. *(Continuous.)*
Or if we do have to continue,
can't we vary the questions a little more
just to alleviate the tedium?
I mean, it's not as though I'm supposed to —
(Stops. Looks at Enright.)
Oh...!
(Pause. Takes this in. Crosses to pick up his coat.)
ENRIGHT.
Charles.

CHARLES.
I won't say anything to anyone.
ENRIGHT.
It's how things are done —
CHARLES.
Not the way I do them.
ENRIGHT.
I just want you to succeed —
CHARLES.
I know that:
Are you expecting me to fail?
ENRIGHT.
I'm expecting you to *triumph!*
But, Charles,
you've said it yourself —
Somewhere on this spherical perplexity
we call earth
there are some
tidbits of information
some *tiniest* facts
that you haven't mastered —
CHARLES.
That's the chance I was supposed to be —
ENRIGHT.
We don't *take* chances here.
Charles.
FREEDMAN. *(Offstage.)*
Dan — Jack wants to talk to you!
(Enright quickly stashes cards in desk drawer. Jack Barry enters, followed by Freedman.)
BARRY.
Danny. Hi.
I was wondering —
do you have any more of those *Cubanos?*
Oh. Hi.
ENRIGHT.
Jack Barry.
Charles Van Doren.

BARRY.
Hello.
ENRIGHT.
Mr. Van Doren is going to be on our show.
BARRY.
Oh,
grand.
I–hope–we–can–help–improve–your–lot–but–of–course–that's–
    up–to–you.
Danny — the cigars?
ENRIGHT.
I'm fresh out, sorry.
Tell Doris to order them.
BARRY.
Damn.
(He exits.)
CHARLES.
You stashed the cards when he came in.
ENRIGHT.
Charles —
FREEDMAN.
Does he — ?
ENRIGHT.
Yes.
CHARLES.   *(Simultaneous with above.)*
Your own partner doesn't know what's —
ENRIGHT.
Charles, listen.
Jack is ...
Well, how do you explain Jack, Al?
FREEDMAN.
He's ...
ENRIGHT.
Jack's ...
Not everyone is intelligent, Charles.
Jack is a very sweet man,
a very *dear* man,
but things to him are what they are.

CHARLES.
Is that how you define stupidity?
ENRIGHT.
Oh, Charlie,
this is not some big moral stand
you're taking —
this is a failure to grasp the medium.
This is entertainment, Charles.
Entertainment requires calculation.
It's that simple.
The other day you said
you wanted to help preserve certain values with this
— and I thought that was the most important part of it for
 you —
maybe I was wrong.
But if I wasn't wrong,
what can possible *disturb* you here?
We're not breaking any rules,
it will be the best thing for *everyone* —
so what is it that *scares* you here? ...
Is it just that it's likely
to have an effect?
(Pause.)
CHARLES.
Who would know?
ENRIGHT.
The three of us.
(Beat.)
CHARLES.
The guy you've got going now —
ENRIGHT.
Mr. Stempel.
CHARLES.
Mr. Stempel.
Was he ... arranged
as well?
ENRIGHT.
Obviously, I can't *tell* you that.

CHARLES.
Would he know about ... his successor?
ENRIGHT.
He won't be a problem.
Nobody will know anything.
You'll come to our offices.
You'll have your sessions
of advice and encouragement
usually, I think, with Mr. Freedman;
you'll be ...
two people alone in a room.
(Beat.)
CHARLES.
I'm sorry
I understand what you're saying but
I just don't —
ENRIGHT.
Think about it.
CHARLES.
I ...
Yes
all right.
ENRIGHT.
Take your time
CHARLES.
Thank you.
ENRIGHT.
but not too much
and Charles?
(Charles looks at him.)
The *choice* is yours;
but the *necessity* lies elsewhere.
(Charles exits.)
FREEDMAN.
What the fuck did that mean?
ENRIGHT.   *(Lights. Music starts low — something lush and fifties. Enright solo.)*
And so Charles went away

and this is what I imagine:
That during those few days
the offer I'd made him
was the only thing he could think of.
That it kept him up
into the small hours of the morning
and drove him into the city streets
where for the first time he looked
really *looked*
at that world from which he'd always politely turned away:
a world of toasters and furs and cars and skin creams
and dimmers and Miltown and cocktail shakers and TV sets —
a gorgeousness of *things*.
And at some moment he didn't notice,
I suspect the question changed for him,
became no longer what he would *do*,
but how he was to *think* of it.
And my guess is that this happened:
He remembered what he'd been teaching with such difficulty
the first time he'd come to see me.
And from that enormous confusion,
I think Charles was attracted to a single idea:
You can behave any way at all in the world
as long as God has whispered in your ear
that you're of the Elect.
Because if you've been chosen
what you do *must* be right — deep down, privately, obscurely
    right —
no matter how it seems — it only follows —
Anything can mean anything — how delightful! How free!
What he said to himself about this was:
"I will lie in service to the truth of the mind."
He said to himself:
"It's such a big paradox."
One condition:
(Charles is with Enright now.)
CHARLES.
I don't want you to give me the answers.

ENRIGHT.
I don't understand.
CHARLES.
Just give me the questions.
ENRIGHT.
Charlie —
CHARLES.
It's the only way I'll do this —
You don't have to worry;
I'm rather good at this sort of thing.
(Beat.)
ENRIGHT.
As you wish.
CHARLES.
I'll do the research myself.
The hard work.
It'll be like
... school.
(Lights. Title: Mr. Van Doren Makes His Debut. Twenty-One: Stempel and Charles in booths; Jack Barry at podium. Gradually, lights drain, projections fill in. Enright, Freedman, Sponsor, Network watching. Projection(s): Charles.)
BARRY.
Just out of curiosity,
Mr. Van Doren,
are you in any way related to Mark Van Doren
up at Columbia University,
the famous writer?
CHARLES.
Yes.
I am.
He is my father.
BARRY.
He is your father!
CHARLES.
Yes.
SPONSOR. *(Overlapped.)*
Now *this* guy, for example,

someone like *this* guy —
He would be *helpful.*
BARRY.
The name Van Doren is a very well-known name.
Are you related to any of the other well-known Van Dorens?
FREEDMAN.
God, I hope he wins ...
CHARLES.
Well, Dorothy Van Doren,
the novelist and author of the recent *The Country Wife*
is my mother,
and Carl Van Doren, the biographer of Benjamin Franklin,
was my uncle.
And my aunt, Carl's wife, Irita Van Doren,
was an editor of the *Nation,*
as was my mother.
NETWORK.
What's he like, Dan?
BARRY. *(Overlapped.)*
Well, you have every reason in the world
to be proud of your name and family:
Van Doren.
ENRIGHT.
Not so interesting.
(Light change.)
BARRY.
And it's a tie!
Congratulations, Mr. Stempel!
Congratulations, Mr. Van Doren!
SPONSOR.
Well, that's encouraging.
FREEDMAN.
Isn't it?
SPONSOR.
Wouldn't it be great
if we finally had a nice, wholesome champion
instead of this, you know, freak with a trick brain?

ENRIGHT.
God — I really hope he wins next week.
SPONSOR.
God — I really hope he does.
(Coaching scene. Coaching: Enright and Stempel.)
STEMPEL.
Catherine Howard was beheaded
chop-chop.
ENRIGHT.
No chop-chop.
Daub your lips.
STEMPEL.
Anne Boleyn
was beheaded, too,
chop-chop.
ENRIGHT.
Herb!
STEMPEL.
Jeez — why are you so testy?
I'm just trying to inject a note of levity.
ENRIGHT.
We don't have time for levity.
STEMPEL.
I think my demeanor
has been a little grim of late.
ENRIGHT.
That's not a problem.
STEMPEL.
And, you know,
you want to keep yourself fresh for the people
so ...
ENRIGHT.
That won't be necessary.
All right, the category is —
STEMPEL.
Can I ask you something?
ENRIGHT.
No.

STEMPEL.
Am I going to tie again this week?
(Beat. Enright stares at him reprovingly.)
I realize that
this is the sort of question
I have been trained not to ask
but, you see,
last week, when it happened,
I think I looked rattled,
I think it seemed out of *char*acter
and if it happens again
I'd like to be able to register
the appropriate emotion
so, um,
am I going to tie
with him
again?
ENRIGHT.
... You don't have to worry about tying, Herb.
STEMPEL.
Good.
... Wait. What does that mean?
ENRIGHT.
The category is "Movies and Movie Stars":
At this point, you will be asked to name
the Academy Award winner
for "Best Picture of 1955."
You will reply —
STEMPEL.
Marty.
ENRIGHT.
You will reply —
STEMPEL.
Marty —
It went to *Marty.*
Or they woulda had *me* to answer to.
It oughta go to *Marty* every year
in my opinion.

ENRIGHT.
You will reply, *On the Waterfront.*
STEMPEL.
What?
ENRIGHT.
It will be an incorrect reply.
STEMPEL.
Hey —
ENRIGHT.
We will then move on to Mr. Van Doren —
STEMPEL.
Hey —
ENRIGHT.
He'll answer whatever he answers, then —
STEMPEL.
Hey, hey, hey,
time out, mister.
Answer me one thing.
ENRIGHT.
...What?
(Beat.)
STEMPEL.
Is this the question?
Because ... last week ... I got the feeling that ...
I mean ... is this gonna be my K.O. punch?
ENRIGHT.
Herb.
STEMPEL.
Tell me please.
(Beat.)
ENRIGHT.
You've had a good run, Herb.
(Pause.)
STEMPEL.
Already?
ENRIGHT.
... Okay.
We will then move on to Mr. Van Doren —

STEMPEL.
You're gonna do it to me on *Marty*?
Marty?
ENRIGHT.
Herb, I have a meeting with Mr. Barry in half-an-hour;
I can't waste time talking about —
STEMPEL.
No, wait a minute, there's something you don't understand —
You see, *Marty* is my favorite movie.
Marty — I love *Marty*.
ENRIGHT.
All the same —
STEMPEL.
No, wait, you see,
Marty's a sort of ... this guy who
He's really a wonderful character and
And I loved the Rod Steiger version, too,
on the Philco-General Electric Playhouse,
with Nancy Marchand in the Betsy Blair role
— she seemed even more realistic —
ENRIGHT.
We really have to move on with —
STEMPEL. *(Over.)*
So when you ask me to take a *dive* on *Marty*
it's just not possible.
I mean — it's close to my heart.
It's close to my —
ENRIGHT.
Listen, Herb, that's the question —
STEMPEL.
All right, fine, no problem!
Ask the same question — change the *year!*
I'll lie about a movie
(though I know every Oscar winner ever
and I mean back to *Wings*).
But it can't be *this* movie.
That's all.
Please.

I have no particular fondness for *The Greatest Show on Earth*.
(Beat.)
ENRIGHT.
You will be asked to name the Best Picture of 1955;
you will reply —
STEMPEL.
Wait a minute! ...
Why are you doing this to me?
ENRIGHT.
Herb —
STEMPEL.
This is such a little thing I'm asking for
but it *matters* —
ENRIGHT.
This is not acceptable.
STEMPEL.
How could this not be acceptable?
We're on the same side.
ENRIGHT.
You will be asked to name the Best Picture of —
STEMPEL.
I've been an exceptionally good champion!
I've been very obedient to the situation.
I was hoping to tell *stories* to my *son* about this —
this is not the story I was hoping to tell
but I've done everything you asked
so how can you not —
ENRIGHT.
Herb —
STEMPEL.
I mean, I've worn these clothes.
I've answered incorrectly
innumerable answers I had at my fingertips.
I've even pretended to people
you actually pay as much as you say you do — no small thing —
ENRIGHT.
Herb, listen —

STEMPEL. *(Continuous.)*
I mean, I've gone into that *booth*
week after week
I've sweated and I've stuttered
and I've been deferential and I've never told a joke
or smiled nicely or done anything but what you asked of me.
I mean, I've done every single thing you asked of —
I've done every —
I've done
I've done ...
What have I done?
ENRIGHT.
Herb.
STEMPEL.
... Let me play straight.
ENRIGHT.
Christ!
STEMPEL.
Scrap everything!
One night —
give me just one night — !
I'll — whatever — I'll
give back all the money
but let me play for real
because it can't
I can't have it end like this —
ENRIGHT.
We have established rules, Herb.
Mr. Barry has *seen* these questions.
What explanation
what explanation
do you propose we give Mr. Barry?
I don't know how it is where you grew up
but around here when a man gives his word
we expect him to keep it.
You gave your word, Herb.
This little
this sentimental explosion

this *Marty* crap —
it's crap.
Now I think a man *is* his word.
The question is:
are *you* that kind of man?
Are you your word, Herb?
When you're in that isolation booth
can I expect cooperation?
Are you *contented* with this?
(Long pause.)
STEMPEL.   *(Very softly.)*
I'm content.
(Pause.)
ENRIGHT.
Okay ...
Oh, come on, Herb — don't look like that.
Listen, I wasn't going to tell you this
but there's a new panel show
Mr. Barry and I are putting together
and who do you think was the first person
we thought of for that panel?
STEMPEL.
I don't know ...
ENRIGHT.
Your wit, your intellect ...
STEMPEL.
Uh-huh.
ENRIGHT.
Won't that be good?
STEMPEL.
I ... yes.
ENRIGHT.
This had to end sometime,
but God, we don't want to lose what you've given us.
Make this a good show, yes?
Look:
I'm glad you're taking this so well.

STEMPEL.
Yes ... well
What Else Can You Do at the End of a Love Affair?
Ha-ha ...
(Enright exits. Special on Stempel, still in chair, staring out as Twenty-One *projections and V.O. come in.)*
BARRY.
Herb Stempel:
For five points which would give you twenty-one,
which motion picture won the Academy Award
for nineteen fifty-five?
STEMPEL.   *(Live.)*
Marty.
(Recorded.)
I don't remember. I don't remember.
BARRY.
You don't want to take a guess at it?
If not, I'll have to call it wrong, Herb.
STEMPEL.   *(Live.)*
Marty?
(Recorded.)
On the Waterfront?
BARRY.
No, I'm sorry,
the answer is *Marty.*
STEMPEL.   *(Recorded.)*
Marty
Oh, *Marty* ...
(Live.)
Oh, *Marty* ...
(As Stempel exits: Stempel projection is replaced by Charles projection. Happy sound event/happy light event.)
BARRY.
Herb Stempel: Thank you for being a wonderful contestant
    and goodbye!
Charles Van Doren: Congratulations on a splendid victory
and come back next week!
Goodnight, ladies and gentlemen,

remember Geritol and Geritol Jr.!
Goodnight and good luck, Charles Van Doren!
(Sound event crescendo. Title: Fourth Victorious Week.
Charles' monologue.)
CHARLES.
Dad:
Why do people still write letters
when there's the telephone?
No one makes silent movies any more.
In any event,
the epistolary art
is alive and well
and centers, it would seem,
upon my tiny, coldwater flat.
A deluge of correspondence these last couple of weeks
from every part of the country,
letters hopeful, praiseful, grateful, extravagant.
About me. Amazing!
Although, by and large,
I find them to be grotesque and mis-spelled —
Re-write:
Although many of the letters
are just typical fan stuff,
every now and then comes one
so eloquent and sincere and kind and well-intentioned
it sends me reeling into a sort of stylish, French abyss —
Re-write:
it makes me truly proud.
I had to hire a girl to answer them this week
because they scare me —
Re-write:
because I'm so busy.
Anyway, there's a lot more money now — would you like some money? —
and the world is moving in a different way
towards me — it's delightful and hectic and with any luck
I'll lose next week.
Maybe I'll throw the contest. Kidding:

Delete.
Finally, in answer to your question:
Yes, you're right.
The moment in the isolation booth when they ask you a question
is the academic's nightmare.
A number of times I've stood there,
uncertain how to respond,
everything hanging in the balance,
and the thought that's gone through my mind has been about you:
"Why didn't you teach me better?"
But that passes and the answer comes.
Don't be proud of my courage — I'm only doing what anyone would do,
after all.
Oh, listen, don't worry —
obviously, this isn't as dire as I'm making it sound —
You know what an *actor* I can be.
STEMPEL. *(Offstage.)*
You LIED!
CHARLES.
Best,
Charles.
(Stempel appears.)
ENRIGHT.
Don't go off your rocker here —
FREEDMAN.
Would you like some coffee, Herb?
STEMPEL.
It's right here in *Variety!*
The cast list for the new Barry-Enright panel show!
My name is nowhere to be —
ENRIGHT.
Do you honestly think
I didn't consider
offer your name for consideration?

STEMPEL.
I have a quick, witty manner
and I wouldn't sweat if the lights weren't so hot —
ENRIGHT.
I was overruled — !
Hear me, Herb!
You were *vetoed.*
Understand?
STEMPEL.
You lie every which way,
To me!
Why?
Am I so...?
Reparations
Restitutions, Mr. Enright.
Costs must be defrayed,
I must be —
ENRIGHT.
If you need me to lend you some *money,* I'd —
STEMPEL.
Money is not what I am after.
ENRIGHT.
Then what is?
STEMPEL.
I want a re-match with Mr. Van Doren.
ENRIGHT.
... Why don't you just let me
give you some money?
STEMPEL.
Played *straight.*
ENRIGHT.
... You know that isn't possible.
STEMPEL.
That's what I —
ENRIGHT.
What would be the basis of it?
What would be the reason?
Herb, please be realistic.

Name something else.
STEMPEL.
You have to give me what I ask for, Mr. Enright,
because I *deserve* it.
(Beat.)
Okay:
Because I possess *information*.
(Beat.)
FREEDMAN.
Would you like a smoke, Herb?
Phillip Morris is experimenting with a new filter-tip for men —
STEMPEL.
I possess information
of a most *significant* nature —
ENRIGHT.
Of course you do.
You don't become a long running champ on *Twenty-One*
if you don't possess information.
Lots of it.
FREEDMAN.
What?
ENRIGHT.
I mean, that's what we picked you for —
STEMPEL.
I can go to the newspapers, Mr. Enright.
Television is not exactly beloved of the newspapers —
What do you think they'd do
if I told them your whole enterprise was rigged?
ENRIGHT.
Rigged —
in what sense, "rigged?"
(Beat.)
STEMPEL.
Okay.
Now what's this,
what game are you playing now?
Is this, what, your strategy?
Have you no shame?

I may be a little shaky
but I'm not without my bearings
and I know damn well that —
ENRIGHT.
Do you know what's most upsetting
to me in this, Herb?
Aside from what you're doing to me
and Mr. Freedman,
the way you're violating every trust we had.
What really disturbs me is
what it's showing me about *you*.
Because I think we've come to be friends,
as I know you'll remember
once you stop being so angry
and I see in you such a terrible *lack,*
such a lack of self-confidence.
STEMPEL.
A lack of self-con —
ENRIGHT.
Don't you believe you could have won on your own?
(Beat.)
STEMPEL.
On my...?
Of *course* I believe it!
It's the thing I believe most in the world!
You *took* that away from —
ENRIGHT.
What have you got against Mr. Van Doren, Herbie?
STEMPEL.
I — what?
... This has nothing to do with him —
ENRIGHT.
This re-match you want — what else could it be
but the desire to get even for imaginary offenses —
STEMPEL.
I have *talent!*
I have *powers!*
... I have my own

(He becomes too upset to speak. A breath.)
I could have won millions!
I'm *owed* that!
And a measure of
esteem ...
the esteem of my peers
the approval of my ...
I want that ... very badly.
ENRIGHT.
But that's a sickness.
(Beat.)
Now how much shall I lend you? What would tide you over?
STEMPEL.
You're dead.
(He exits quickly.)
ENRIGHT.
Herb — !
(No answer. He turns back.)
Don't think about it.
(Lights. Title: The Newspapers. Corso's office at the New York Post. Corso and Stempel.)
STEMPEL.
Mr. Corso, you have to know
I'm not doing this for the publicity factor.
The publicity factor is meaningless to me.
CORSO.   *(Flicking ash from cigarette.)*
Oh, yeah, yeah, yeah, yeah, sure.
STEMPEL.
True, I have some hopes of forging an acting career
but I'm putting that aside for the moment
because
during my *time*
I met with an *agent*
who suggested
it might not be immediately su*stain*ing
until I grow into my type.
Or perhaps it would.
Do you think?

CORSO.
Weeellll!
(A pleasantly non-committal shrug.)
STEMPEL.
Regardless:
this is not that.
This is just
I can't take it any more.
I can't believe what they're doing to me.
I can't believe what *I've* done.
CORSO.
I gotta say
this is some pretty hot stuff.
I mean:
in*cen*diary.
STEMPEL.
Every word is the *emmis!*
I swear to you.
I told friends
— they disregarded me —
the moral stature of the common man,
sad to say, is shockingly low.
I told Spats O'Brian.
You know Spats O'Brian of the *Journal-American.*
CORSO.   *(Overlapped.)*
Sure, from the *Journal-American,* sure —
what did he do with it?
STEMPEL.
He
umm
I don't know
I believe he's still researching.
(Phone rings. Spats O'Brian and Enright appear.)
O'BRIAN.
Mr. Enright —
STEMPEL.
He seemed to me to lack a certain courage —

ENRIGHT.
Yes?
CORSO.
Well, here at the *Post*,
courage we got plenty —
O'BRIAN.
Spats O'Brian here
the *Journal-American*?
We met once at the —
ENRIGHT.
— at the Motorama Show, of course —
what can I do for you?
O'BRIAN.
I think you should know
I had a visit the other day
from Herb Stempel —
STEMPEL.
I will stand by my words
in any court of law
on any affadavit
before God Him*self* —
CORSO.
Cool.
O'BRIAN.
He made some rather
well
shocking remarks —
ENRIGHT.
I see ...
STEMPEL.
I must tell you:
I've pursued other outlets
and not received satisfaction.
But you're the *Press*
and I'm putting my *faith* in you.
(*He exits. Corso stubs out cigarette, starts to dial phone.*)
O'BRIAN.
We did a little research

purely a formality, mind you
and I know there's nothing to it
and God knows I'm not in the market for a libel suit —
but I thought you should be made aware —
ENRIGHT.
Yes, yes, thank you.
(Phone rings.)
Hello?
CORSO.
Mr. Enright?
Warren Corso — New York *Post* —
We met that time, remember?
Coltrane was at the Five Spot —
ENRIGHT.
Yes, yes, of course —
O'BRIAN.
My reporter's instincts
told me immediately
it was no story —
CORSO.
So the other day
this most peculiar cat
cat by the name of Herbert Stempel
comes into my office
tells me this story
— crazy stuff —
but I don't hold by this cat's tale
and you know why?
O'BRIAN.
With Mr. Stempel
the tip-off was *drool.*
CORSO.
*Shoe*laces.
O'BRIAN.
I noticed he was drooling.
CORSO.
I'm lapping up his story
I look down:

his shoes are untied.
O'BRIAN.
And he made no move to wipe it away.
CORSO.
The laces flapping, flapping, flapping —
O'BRIAN.
So you're safe —
CORSO.
I said to myself,
"No sale, baby."
O'BRIAN.
But I thought you should know.
ENRIGHT.
Poor Herb.
Poor Mr. Stempel.
O'BRIAN.
What do you mean?
CORSO. *(Simultaneous with above.)*
How's that?
ENRIGHT.
The sad fact is
Mr. Stempel is a madman.
O'BRIAN.
Really?
CORSO. *(Simultaneous.)*
God*damn!*
O'BRIAN. *(Continuos.)*
Has he been diagnosed as such
by a professional man?
ENRIGHT.
Now look
I'm not in the habit
of vilifying my performers.
I like them as a rule.
In fact, I like Herb Stempel.
I feel paternal towards him.
And perhaps "mad" is too strong a word.
Are you familiar with

the idea of "Jewish self-hatred"?
O'BRIAN and CORSO. *(Unison.)*
Sure.
ENRIGHT.
Well,
Mr. Stempel is so consumed with it
that he can't stand to succeed.
It throws him completely out-of-whack.
This is his way of restoring psychological equilibrium.
Slandering *us* is only incidental.
The one he really hopes to slander is *himself.*
O'BRIAN.
A-a-h! *F-a-a-a*-scinating.
CORSO. *(From "F-a-a-a-a.")*
This is some sick, crazy jazz you're blowing me.
ENRIGHT.
Now
I wouldn't dream
of interfering with your work
any more than *you'd* dream
of interfering with mine —
But I implore you:
Be discreet.
I'm very protective of my own.
O'BRIAN.
Of course.
CORSO. *(Simultaneously.)*
You got it.
O'BRIAN.
And by the way:
Congratulations on that
Van Doren fellow!
My wife and I are
riveted —
CORSO. *(Over "riveted.")*
Man,
that egghead is *scramblin'!*
(Lights. Charles in isolation booth.)

CHARLES' VOICE. *(Semi-monotone.)*
Aristotle gave us the idea of the Unities.
Hegel spoke of world-historical figures.
The Superman was the idea of Neitzche.
Dorothy Rodgers invented the Johnny-mop.
Anne Hathaway — sorry, Anne *Hutchinson*
was at the center of the Antinomian Controversy.
(Anne Hathaway was Shakespeare's wife.)
(As tape continues, Charles emerges from booth, gets hat and coat. Enright appears in his office. Late night. He has a drink, he's leaning back with his legs up on the desk, obviously exhausted.)
St. Augustine said, "Love means that I want you to be."
Mae West said, "Come up and see me sometime."
Ina Rae Hutton is Betty Hutton's sister.
It was Heidegger who wrote, "The light of the public always obscures."
The encyclopedia was invented by Diderot.
(By this time, Charles has crossed to Enright's office. He hovers there uncertainly for a moment.)
CHARLES.
... Excuse me?
ENRIGHT.
Charlie
Oh
Hi
CHARLES.
Are you in the middle of — ?
ENRIGHT.
Not at all.
Come on in.
Have a drink.
Sit down.
CHARLES.
Thanks.
(As Enright pours the drinks:)
You look tired.
ENRIGHT.
Bone-tired.

Long week.
... Here you go.
CHARLES.
Thank you.
ENRIGHT.
Now:
What do you want from me?
CHARLES.
Oh God,
nothing.
Does everybody always want something from you?
ENRIGHT.
Yes.
CHARLES.
... Just the drink, thanks.
ENRIGHT.
... Sure.
(Beat.)
Take your time....
You did very well tonight, Charles.
CHARLES.
Did very well
um
how could I help myself?
ENRIGHT.
No, I mean the by-play
the sweating —
much improved.
CHARLES.
Oh ... that.
ENRIGHT.
Did you read that article by the way?
The Atlantic Monthly.
It said you've "grown" over these past weeks.
You were "callow" at first
but now there's an "ambivalence" to your "demeanor"
as though you're worrying about how much
"beauty" can give up to "commodity"

— something like that —
It said you've taken on an aura of almost "presidential density."
This is very good, Charles.
CHARLES.
... Yes.
(Beat.)
I want to stop.
(Beat.)
ENRIGHT.
No.
CHARLES.
Please listen —
ENRIGHT.
You're having an enormous success, Charlie;
of course you're miserable.
CHARLES.
It isn't that.
ENRIGHT.
Sure it is.
Who's had more experience at this
you or —
CHARLES.
If you'd just stop understanding me
and *listen* ...
(Pause.)
I'm sorry
... but you have to know
I'm not just being capricious here. Dan;
this isn't some
easy
"crisis of conscience" I'm indulging ...
I'm finding it almost literally impossible
to make my way through a day with this....
Everything
the most unimportant things
require the most incredible calculation
and I don't know how to manage it.
... I can't figure what to say

or what to conceal
or which lies make sense
and when I'm not lying at all
it feels like an oversight ...
ENRIGHT.
On the show you're doing very —
CHARLES.
On the show it's worse.
... I'm asked these questions
and even when I've known the stuff forever
none of it is ... familiar, somehow —
You've seen it —
there are times I can barely stammer out the answers
ENRIGHT. *(Under.)*
That works.
CHARLES. *(Continuous.)*
as though it's all become some other thing ... do you see?
Because I've *made* it that.
And I can't stand it.
(Beat; quietly.)
Or any of it.
... The whole thing ... all the time ...
... I feel as though I've violated some sort of
covenant
I never even knew I made
but without it,
I don't know how to go on.
(Beat; no answer.)
Dan?
ENRIGHT.
Okay, Charles, look,
the fact is,
we have an agreement, you and I —
CHARLES.
But why does it have to go on so long?
ENRIGHT.
It goes *on* because it is under*way* —
Look, give this time, will you?

CHARLES.
Giving it time is what I'm most afraid of —
ENRIGHT.
Trust me.
Time will *demolish*
everything unpleasant about this, Charlie.
A few months from now
this will be like
the memory of a *memory*
and you will see
that all of it
— the whole affair —
has been nothing, nothing at all
— a show....
Oh, look, Charlie,
your life isn't so *bad*.
Maybe you've had a couple of tough moments
in public.
Maybe some people at Columbia have said insulting things —
well of course they have, they're your colleagues —
but you're *famous* —
That's good, no matter what it feels like.
And there may not be much money now
but believe me
there *will* be
and all sorts of opportunities —
CHARLES.
I won't want them —
ENRIGHT.
Yes you will
and
I read in a magazine
— I had to read it in a magazine —
you're even seeing that pretty girl,
the one who answers your fan mail
she looks awfully nice.
CHARLES.
She's wonderful, yes.

ENRIGHT.
There you are.
CHARLES. *(Overlaps.)*
But I can't talk to her.
ENRIGHT.
Who can ever talk to a twenty-three-year-old girl, Charlie?
CHARLES.
Because I can't talk about *this*
and this is everything.
ENRIGHT.
You're a good man.
CHARLES.
That changes so quickly.
ENRIGHT.
But it hasn't changed in *this*.
CHARLES.
Please — Listen to — I don't want to win any more.
ENRIGHT.
Tough:
It's your fate.
(Beat.)
Do you know what's happened, Charlie?
Because of *you*
Do you know
u-u-h
how many requests for college applications
have been filed in these last weeks?
That alone.
There's been a run on the printers —
we got something in about it just today —
because of you.
Now you can tell me
you "expected" something
and "things" have become other "things" —
That's completely abstract — take it to Columbia —
I don't know about that.
But what I *do* know is this:
You said you wanted to do good.

That good is just beginning.
Are you going to take
all the honor out of this thing?
I mean, really,
how many covenants are you planning to break?
(Beat.)
You've made it through seven weeks of this.
A couple more
they'll pass like that.
Now.
I am going home
and getting some sleep
Coming?
CHARLES.
... Yes.
ENRIGHT.
You look like hell.
I'll wait with you till you find a cab.
CHARLES.
I can get my own cab.
ENRIGHT.
... Whatever you say.
(He picks up his coat and starts out.)
CHARLES.
Do you think— ?
ENRIGHT.
What?
CHARLES.
Do you think
we only recognize grace
once we've fallen from it?
ENRIGHT.
I have absolutely no idea, Charlie.
(Charles looks at him. Exiting.)
Good night.
(Charles remains. He puts on his coat, then stares straight out, unmoving. Light closes in on him, grows blindingly bright, then quick blackout. Projection: Charles on **Twenty-One** *— whatever will work.)*

BARRY. *(Voice over.)*
Good evening and welcome
to another exciting game of *Twenty-One*.
Tonight we're most pleased
and thrilled as can be
to welcome back our wonderful champion
Charles Van Doren
for an all-time-record
fifteenth consecutive appearance.
Charlie?
(Charles stares straight out. Sound climax.)

End Act One

ACT TWO

In darkness.

TV VOICE.
So, if you're the type who wakes still weary
from the previous day's exertions,
the folks at General Mills have come up with a cure
for your morning malady:
Breakfast Power — the Cornflakes with Caffeine!
You need never be sleepy again ...
Now back to Dave Garroway and *The Today Show* ...
(Projection: The Today Show.)
DAVE GARROWAY.
Thank you, Frank.
It's twenty-two minutes after the hour
and we have a new feature here on *The Today Show*.
I'm sure you all remember Charles Van Doren
from his unprecedented four month run
on the *Twenty-One* program
not so many months ago.
Well
we've been fortunate enough to procure
Mr. Van Doren
to come in from time to time
and talk about books
and matters of cultural import
and so forth.
Welcome to the show, Charlie.
(Fade in: Toby transfixed before the TV, bathed in its light. Stempel comes up behind her, staring at her, then at the TV.)
CHARLES.
Thank you, Dave,
and good morning.
Although in general

I should like to use this spot
to discuss poetry and classical works,
this morning
I wish to speak
of something brand new,
a play which can be seen
on the Broadway stage now
in fact
but one which I think
is bound in time
to be regarded as a beloved classic:
STEMPEL.
Middle of the Night
by Paddy Chayefsky!
CHARLES.
J.B.
by Archibald MacLeish.
(Chord. Lights. Enright's office. Enright still in his coat. Freedman bursts in.)
FREEDMAN.
Jesus!
Did you hear about this yet?
ENRIGHT.
Al, it's the crack of dawn.
I haven't had coffee yet.
Can't you at least say good morning
like a person?
FREEDMAN.
Good morning.
Jesus!
Did you hear about this yet?
ENRIGHT.   *(Sighs.)*
... What?
FREEDMAN.
I just had breakfast with Morty Ryman,
you remember Morty, from *Do You Trust Your Wife?*
ENRIGHT.
No.

FREEDMAN.
Doesn't matter. Anyway,
Morty had dinner last night with Burt Cafferty
— he's stage manager on *Top Dollar* —
and Burt told Morty something that, Dan,
when he told me, I swear to you, I mean, I'm *still* —
ENRIGHT.
What?
FREEDMAN.   *(A warning.)*
Lower your voice.
(Doris enters with coffee.)
DORIS.
Here we are!
ENRIGHT.
Thank you.
DORIS.
Good morning, Mr. Freedman,
how are you today?
FREEDMAN.
Fine Doris, thank you, and you?
DORIS.
Very well, thank you. Isn't it a lovely day out?
FREEDMAN.
Yes, beautiful, isn't it, very brisk, thank you.
(Doris smiles, exits; they watch her go. The instant she's gone.)
Okay.
There is this guy
he was a contestant on *Dotto* —
His name's ... Higelheimer — Hegelmeier — something —
ENRIGHT.
Which is it?
FREEDMAN.
That truly makes no difference —
What *does* is,
he was on the same time as Marie Winn —
I'm sure that you remember Marie Winn —
ENRIGHT.
You're sure that I —

Why would I watch, *Dotto?*
FREEDMAN.
You don't watch, *Dotto?*
ENRIGHT.
It's a quiz show — they're so boring.
FREEDMAN.
She was very popular.
Anyway
according to ... this *Dotto* guy,
one fine day
Marie Winn is sitting in the *Dotto* green room
along with all the *other* contestants
but she ignores the other contestants
because she is too busy
happily-merrily reading from this little notebook she has,
moving her lips.
Time passes, she goes off for her first round
— Miss Genius — !
and leaves the notebook behind.
So Higel ... shmemem.
ENRIGHT.
What's his name?
FREEDMAN. *(Over.)*
Who knows! — God — Why didn't somebody *change* it?
His first name's *Ed.*
Ed decides to steal himself a peek.
He takes the notebook,
sneaks into the wings with it,
and listens while she answers —
finds he can *read* along with her.
ENRIGHT.
Jesus.
FREEDMAN.
Is not so dumb not to get that he's been *duped.*
So he *rips out the page!*
And now this disconsolate shit
he's got *evidence* —
He's taken it to some assistant D.A.

who's an ambitious shit and — well, you can figure the rest.
(A breath; composes himself.)
Needless to say, when Morty told me, I was outraged to
discover such things go on at *Dotto*
but Dan —
ENRIGHT.
It's *Dotto*.
Dotto is not our show
FREEDMAN.
The D.A.'s office has already called *Top Dollar*.
On *The Sixty-Four Thousand Dollar Question*,
they're handing over phone numbers of the contestants who —
ENRIGHT.
The people who've been on our show
are Pillars of their Communities
and they will do everything in their power
to avoid telling the truth —
FREEDMAN.
Not every one of them.
(Beat.)
ENRIGHT.
Oh, Christ, he's
How can you be afraid of him?
He's this little *vahntz* —
He hasn't said anything in —
We haven't heard from him — *no*body's heard from him.
For all practical purposes, he's vanished.
FREEDMAN.
Not into the *Mists* of *Time*.
He has an address — he has a phone number.
We will have to hand *over* his phone number.
And this time, people will be *asking* what he knows.
ENRIGHT.
Be calm.
FREEDMAN.
Television is my *life*.
ENRIGHT.
Don't be pathetic.

FREEDMAN.
Dan —
ENRIGHT.
You have nothing to fear.
I will take care of you.
FREEDMAN.
It gives me the willies when you get nice.
What?
What are we gonna do?
(Pause.)
ENRIGHT.
Penance.
(Lights. Phone rings. Enright on phone. Stempel appears in chair, answers phone.)
STEMPEL.
Hello?
ENRIGHT.
Hello, Herb?
Is that you?
STEMPEL.
Yes ...
who is this?
ENRIGHT.
Dan Enright.
STEMPEL. *(In a small voice.)*
Oh no ...
ENRIGHT.
How are you, Herb?
STEMPEL.
I'm ...
I've been
sort of
sitting here ...
I'm *alone* here ...
Maybe we shouldn't ...
Why are you calling me?
ENRIGHT.
Is it so strange

for one friend to call another
to get back in touch?
STEMPEL.
No.
(Beat.)
Why are you calling me?
ENRIGHT.
I wanted to find out how you are,
what you've been up to.
STEMPEL.
I've been ...
sitting here ...
I
There've been ... events
It's been
rather a difficult ...
We've had some re*ver*ses and
u-u-u-u-h ...
Look, nobody else is here,
maybe we shouldn't —
ENRIGHT.
Are you working?
STEMPEL.
Why are you — ?
I
I had a job.
ENRIGHT.
Great!
Doing what?
STEMPEL.
Umm ...
My wife's uncle ...
An accounting concern ...
I was
part of it
I was
I quit.

ENRIGHT.
I'm sorry.
STEMPEL.
I was the best one there!
ENRIGHT.
I'm sure.
STEMPEL.
First day on the job,
my wife's uncle,
I say to him,
"Well, I better get started."
He says, "No rush, no hurry,
we've got plenty of ample time,
plenty of ample time ..."
I mean ... the mentality!
ENRIGHT.
Not for you.
Not for someone of your gifts.
STEMPEL.
I couldn't take it
I'm sorry
I'm talking like this
I
haven't been talking to many people lately
I ...
Why are you calling me?
ENRIGHT.
Yes, you're right,
this isn't just casual ...
Herb, I have to tell you:
I've felt very bad
about what's happened between us.
It's been preying on me
and I've wanted to make amends.
STEMPEL.
... Amends?
ENRIGHT.
I *have* something for you, Herb.

STEMPEL.
Um —
look —
I think I'd better go —
ENRIGHT.
Herb —
STEMPEL.
Look —
I've been through
a lot this ... past —
I'm
in analysis ... twice a week
medications, pills
I
was in a very pleasant Miltown drift
when you called
as a matter of fact and
I
There are
certain kinds of expectations
I've forsworn
and
(Beat.)
it seems to have
stood me in good stead
to have done so,
so
(Beat.)
What is it you have for me?
ENRIGHT.
I want to tell you —
STEMPEL.
I'm hanging up!
ENRIGHT.
Herb, don't!
STEMPEL.
Please —

ENRIGHT.
I'm not going to tell you what this is
over the phone.
(Beat.)
STEMPEL.
Thank you.
ENRIGHT.
I'd like you to come my office —
STEMPEL.
No ...
ENRIGHT.
As soon as possible,
all right?
STEMPEL.
No ...
ENRIGHT.
We'll chat ...
STEMPEL.
No ...
ENRIGHT.
Look,
I'm not going to pretend
there isn't a big payoff for me.
Your gifts, your mind —
STEMPEL.
Look
I've been trying
I've been trying very hard ...
My doctor.
ENRIGHT.
Herb,
have you been feeling alone?
Is that it?
Have you been feeling that nobody cares?
(Beat.)
STEMPEL.   *(Quietly.)*
Yes.

ENRIGHT.
Think of what I'm doing now, Herb:
I've bridged so much time,
so much trouble —
STEMPEL.
Why are you calling me?
ENRIGHT.
Well,
I guess I must care,
mustn't I?
Or why would I invite you back into my life?
(Beat.)
You see that,
don't you, Herb?
(Pause.)
STEMPEL.
Yes.
ENRIGHT.
Are you coming to my office?
(Pause.)
STEMPEL.
No.
ENRIGHT.
Let me repeat the question:
Are you coming to my office?
(Pause.)
STEMPEL.
Yes.
(Chord. Lights. Enright's office. Enright and Freedman. Stempel enters.)
ENRIGHT.
It's good to see you, Herb.
STEMPEL.
Is it?
FREEDMAN.
You're looking well.
STEMPEL.
My legs are wobbling.

ENRIGHT.
Have a seat.
Would you like a Coke, by the way?
A cup of coffee?
STEMPEL.
No, thank you.
ENRIGHT.
That's perfectly all right.
STEMPEL.
Thank you.
ENRIGHT.
I'll start.
You know why you're here.
Today we want to set things right between us.
To re-establish what's true.
And then to take a little stroll,
a little walk through our future together —
How does that sound?
STEMPEL.
Good
that sounds
I'd like a future
Jeez — my legs!
Have I Stayed Too Long in the Chair?
Ha-ha.
ENRIGHT.
Now I'm not going to tell you everything —
STEMPEL.
Oh, no
no no no —
ENRIGHT.
But there is, it looks like something down the line that appears very, very promising.
STEMPEL.
And I want to say
before we go on
that I've mulled this over —

ENRIGHT.
Yes —
STEMPEL.
After your call I mulled it over
very
with great *clarity* —
ENRIGHT.
Uh-huh —
STEMPEL.
And I've concluded that this is a good thing.
ENRIGHT.
I'm *glad*.
STEMPEL.
Deep inside I've always known
that I have the potential to be a commercial entity
and you
you recognize that.
I'm not destined for an ordinary life
and you *understand* that.
ENRIGHT.   *(Over from "I'm not destined.")*
Of course we do.
Of course we do.
And we're going to get to that in a moment.
But first there's something I'd like you to do for me.
STEMPEL.
Sure.
Anything.
ENRIGHT.
In view of certain irregularities
in the past —
STEMPEL.
Anything —
ENRIGHT.
I want you to write a statement now
to the effect that
contrary to what you have said in the past
Dan Enright has at no point
disclosed questions,

answers,
points,
anything like it.
Would you do that for me?
Herb?
(Long pause. Stempel looks back and forth between Enright and Freedman.)
STEMPEL.
I'll be glad to.
(Enright hands Stempel paper and pen. Stempel writes.)
ENRIGHT.   *(Watching the paper.)*
You know
after your last
... visit ...
my lawyer recommended
I take it to the D.A.
But I said,
No — I don't want to destroy this man,
I have affection for this man.
When you left me that day
that terrible day
you made those awful charges
my instinct was to *help* you.
I thought maybe *I* was the one who needed the shrink.
Just sign at the bottom.
Yes.
Thank you.
STEMPEL.
I didn't know who I was.
ENRIGHT.
Excuse me?
STEMPEL.
I know, I said to myself, you know,
Dan he gave you a break, you should be grateful but ... I flipped
I
That thing I got involved in
It was a very bad

a very wasteful
a heart-rending thing
— gambling — a syndicate —
He
I gave him my money
this guy this scary this
guy ... my *neigh*bor
There's no one I could tell this to
I wanted to tell someone.
ENRIGHT.
Sure.
STEMPEL.
I
One day
I come home
and he's gone
ab*scond*ed
with all my money ...
My wife ... I think she was fond of him
I definitely think she was fond of him.
And she had some hopes of moving, of Florida ... and then: this.
She's always been a fearful type,
now — nothing.
We
She sits all day in front of the TV set
watching ...
She never misses *The Today Show*.
ENRIGHT.
It's all right, Herb.
STEMPEL.
I mean, I *know* things
I've *learned* things
I have a *wealth* of information
... So, tell me, with all these wonderful things,
why can't I make the world move an *inch* in my direction?
ENRIGHT.
I want to get you a psychiatrist.

STEMPEL.
I already have one — I *told* you that.
ENRIGHT.
No sir,
I want to get you a psychiatrist five times a week,
not twice.
Because, Herb,
I think you're in the grips of some very bad dreams.
And the opposite of dreams is facts.
And we want to *escort* you
back to the world of facts.
FREEDMAN.
That's all we want.
STEMPEL.
My psychiatrist says I'm my father's fault —
ENRIGHT.
Don't be taken in by the dreams anymore, Herb.
Will you promise me that?
As a friend?
STEMPEL.
He died when I was only —
ENRIGHT.
Facts may not glitter
but they're your *defenders,*
your happiness.
STEMPEL.
Happiness, mm-hm.
FREEDMAN.
Gather your rosebuds ...
STEMPEL.
Yes.
ENRIGHT.
No more dreams.
Now
for the other part of today's meeting:
STEMPEL.
You've found a venue and an occasion and you've scheduled
a re-match between myself and Mr. Van Doren — !

(Beat.)
ENRIGHT.
No.
FREEDMAN.
... Uh
no
that's not
STEMPEL.
Oh
FREEDMAN.
That's not it —
STEMPEL.
A guess, a conjecture, go on ...
ENRIGHT.
This is what it is:
We
Al and I and Mr. Barry
and the network
are planning a new panel show —
okay, yes, *another* panel show —
that's all I can say about it!
Except that this time
there's going to be a berth for you
on that panel.
STEMPEL.
Oh, that would be —
ENRIGHT.
You'd appear once a show;
every day on the air —
STEMPEL.
That would be —
ENRIGHT.
We'd cut to your face;
you'd say a few words —
STEMPEL.
That would be —
ENRIGHT.
You'd be referred to by name

when the occasion arose —
STEMPEL.
My name?
ENRIGHT.
We'd exploit your mind,
your talent —
STEMPEL.
Will you pay my bills?
ENRIGHT.
I
Which bills are we speaking of now?
STEMPEL.
My
All
I bought a car — ?
ENRIGHT.
Oh, Herb.
STEMPEL.
I was walking
I was just walking ...
There was a showplace ...
The car
A three-toned Packard —
ENRIGHT.
Herb, we understand —
STEMPEL.   *(Becoming belligerent.)*
And why shouldn't I have a nice car?
Why shouldn't I have all those things?
I was supposed to
There were promises
Don't look at me like
greed
or or
bad values ...
this sick world!
sick
criminal — !
I just want what's coming to me!

I — !
Oh, Dan, I'm sorry, I'm sorry, I'm so sorry —
It's my fault —
Everything's my fault.
(He cries. Pause. Enright puts his arm around Stempel's shoulder.)
ENRIGHT.
This is not a day for whose fault it is.
The world is hard
and fame can be very harsh.
We opened that door for you
and then it closed
without warning.
I don't think you can cope with life at this stage, Herb.
And I say we have help.
STEMPEL.
I'm perfectly willing to need help.
ENRIGHT.
Good boy.
Well.
This has been an excellent day.
We've made real progress.
The details we'll work out next time.
STEMPEL.
Dan — !
I
It's
People
So many people have
It's gotten to such a point
I
I need someone to trust
... so, don't laugh, I'm choosing you.
All right?
(Beat.)
Is that all right?
ENRIGHT.
I'm
I'll be honored to be the one you trust, Herb.

(Stempel nods, exits. Enright opens desk drawer, removes tape recorder, rewinds, plays. It plays back a portion of their conversation. He turns off the machine. Voice over: "I'm perfectly willing to need help!"*)*
Excellent sound.
(Chord/lights. Fans appear.)
STALWART FAN.
Dear Mr. Van Doren
MORE STALWART FAN.
My dear Mr. Van Doren
GINGERLY FAN.
Dear Mr. Van Doren
STALWART FAN.
Besieged as we are every day
MORE STALWART FAN.
Overwhelmed as we constantly are by reports of Grand Juries
STALWART FAN.
Congressional Committees
MORE STALWART FAN.
taking away the pleasure we had in
The Sixty-Four Thousand Dollar Question
STALWART FAN.
The Sixty-Four Thousand Dollar Challenge
MORE STALWART FAN.
Tic-tac-Dough
STALWART FAN.
Name That Tune
MORE STALWART FAN.
Top Dollar
STALWART FAN.
And so forth
MORE STALWART FAN.
ad infinitum
STALWART FAN.
It's good to know that amidst all this squalor
MORE STALWART FAN.   *(Overlaps.)*
It's heartening to know
that amidst all this turpitude

STALWART FAN. *(Overlaps.)*
You remain an island of
MORE STALWART FAN. *(Overlaps.)*
You remain a bastion of
GINGERLY FAN. *(Tenderly.)*
Dear Charles ... *(Fans clear.)*
(Charles is seated D.C., smoking. The Investigator sits at some distance from Charles, at a skewed angle facing partially U.)
CHARLES.
Hm
Let me see ...
Catherine Parr was ...
oh, I don't know,
beheaded or a suicide
or she overdosed on Bayer aspirin.
And ... u-u-h
Catherine of Aragon, was it?
Didn't she die of old age?
Anne of Cleves ...
I'm sorry
I can't seem to answer your question.
INVESTIGATOR.
Isn't that peculiar?
CHARLES.
I've never been a big fan of regicide.
INVESTIGATOR.
And yet when these questions
were posed to you on *Twenty-One*
you had no problem.
And the other questions, too.
Mr. Van Doren,
I'm afraid I have to ask this:
Have you suffered some sort of
injury to the brain in these last two years?
CHARLES.
Well,
I've been watching more *tele*vision
than I used to,

if that's what you ... but no —
my brain remains as it was —
should I say, "alas?"
INVESTIGATOR.
Then how do you explain
this really rather staggering loss of information?
CHARLES.
Here it is:
You see
it occurred to me soon after I started
that I was unlikely to be asked the same question twice
— it didn't take Sherlock Holmes —
I devised a system:
Once some information was extracted from me,
I deleted it from my memory bank.
I created a sort of mental space for the information
from which I was more likely to derive profit.
Not to brag,
but the system seems to have worked.
INVESTIGATOR.
For many of you people from *Twenty-One*
it seems;
I mean,
I've heard the same sort of thing
from a lot of you from *Twenty-One*.
CHARLES.
Oh ...
Trick minds think alike, too, I guess —
INVESTIGATOR.   *(Overlaps.)*
So then what this system
boils down to
is a sort of
self-induced intellectual amnesia.
CHARLES.
Yes.
Well put.
INVESTIGATOR.
And do you ever miss what you've forgotten?

CHARLES.
I
(Beat.)
I'm sorry
No one's ever asked that question before.
INVESTIGATOR. *(Soothingly.)*
That's all right.
CHARLES.
Um
May *I* ask something.
INVESTIGATOR.
Certainly.
CHARLES.
Why is this happening?
INVESTIGATOR.
I beg your —
CHARLES.
I mean,
that whole grand jury thing I had to endure
and now *Con*gress steps in —
INVESTIGATOR.
Well: Television —
just burgeoning, really, isn't it?
Whenever there's a new concentration of power in society
the job is to determine the appropriate restraints.
With these hearings —
CHARLES.
Yes, yes, yes
I get all that
and by all means if there's been some sort of corruption
among these other shows,
expose it, reveal it!
But with *Twenty-One* it seems to me
all you have are the allegations of a man
universally agreed to be *mad*.
And *he's* retracted them!
That statement he —

INVESTIGATOR.
Mr. Stempel claims
he was tricked into signing that —
CHARLES.
But the tape —
INVESTIGATOR.
We've listened to that tape.
CHARLES.
Then you *know*.
INVESTIGATOR.
We hear edits.
(Beat.)
CHARLES.
Nevertheless, a madman.
At least that's what I'm told.
I barely know him myself.
Listen, I'm not interested in slandering anyone here,
but since the only one accusing anyone is bananas
and with, it would appear, a psychotic, motivelessly malignant
vendetta against me, it doesn't —
INVESTIGATOR.
Mr. Stempel *is* pretty adamant we bring you up
before the committee,
calls all the time —
CHARLES.
I know.
INVESTIGATOR. *(Continuous.)*
But he's not the only accuser, is he?
CHARLES.
I —
INVESTIGATOR. *(With a shuffle of paper.)*
I mean, we've got,
well, there *is* that one guy in your department
said, "Charlie couldn't have known all those things;
Charlie barely knows his own subject" —
CHARLES.
Someone ... *who* said — ?

INVESTIGATOR. *(Continuous.)*
but that's just
what that is — however,
there's also that minister
who confessed to his congregation
what he'd been part of on *Twenty-One* —
The Reverend, uh, Reverend —
CHARLES.
The Reverend Reverend
yes, I know who you —
INVESTIGATOR.
Why would a minister lie?
CHARLES. *(Testy.)*
I don't know.
Maybe he's uncomfortable with games of chance.
Maybe they make him feel like a Catholic.
(Apologetic half-smile.)
Sorry.
INVESTIGATOR. *(Soothingly.)*
That's all right.
CHARLES.
... Yes.
INVESTIGATOR.
What, "yes?"
CHARLES.
I do sometimes miss what I've forgotten.
INVESTIGATOR.
Oh.
CHARLES.
I miss a lot of things ... in fact.
INVESTIGATOR.
I'm sure.
CHARLES. *(Continuous.)*
A lot of this thing
has been pretty hellish
to tell the truth and
I really don't know how much longer I can ...
I've done nothing wrong,

you see.
Unless it's wrong to
go on television
and teach people about literature.
Or to inspire people
to continue their education.
I don't know — maybe it is wrong — I can't see it
... But how do I persuade anyone?
Do I list my accomplishments?
I could say,
Well, look, I've done this and this and this
but what would it matter
now that there's this
aura around everything.
Even here. This.
You've been tremendously polite
but you mistrust me, it's the worst thing,
and it's everywhere.
Cordial-seeming people who get very suddenly quiet when they —
I mean, people more-or-less *evaporate* in my presence and that's —
Even those ... who absolutely believe me
even the people *nearest* to me —
Are you married?
INVESTIGATOR.
Yes.
CHARLES.
My wife
is the nicest girl I know.
And the smartest.
We discuss
the Carolingian poets
... when we're being especially close.
INVESTIGATOR.
Mr. Van Doren —
CHARLES.
I've done absolutely nothing wrong,

why isn't that enough?
And I don't mean simply the *facts* of the thing,
that's part of it,
but there's so much else besides the facts,
so much else
that no one ever seems to take into account —
my *intentions*, my reasons,
the ... rightness
the rightness *beyond* rightness of my reasons,
nobody ever seems to ask about that or consider
what it may —
INVESTIGATOR.   *(From "seems to ask.")*
What does that mean?
CHARLES.
...What?
INVESTIGATOR.
You just said something about
"the rightness beyond rightness of your reasons" —
I don't understand what that means.
(Pause.)
CHARLES.   *(Quietly.)*
Why should you?
It's babble.
INVESTIGATOR.
... Ah ...
CHARLES.
... I'm having some trouble lately ...
matching words to my life.
(Pause. Charles smiles at Investigator; it's incredibly sad.)
This has been
an unnecessary sneak preview of my breakdown.
I'm sorry; I haven't been sleeping.
INVESTIGATOR.
That's all right.
CHARLES.   *(Checks his watch.)*
The time.
... I have to go.
I need to get back to Columbia now and

... natter things at sophomores —
INVESTIGATOR.
That's all right;
I'll be calling you again very soon.
CHARLES.
Of course.
INVESTIGATOR.
Mr. Van Doren — before you go — may I ask a favor of you?
CHARLES.
What's that?
INVESTIGATOR.
Would you say hello to your father for me?
CHARLES.
... What?
INVESTIGATOR.
He was my teacher centuries ago.
CHARLES.
Is that right?
INVESTIGATOR.
I don't know why I think he'd remember me
except
he has a talent for making the most unexceptional person
feel memorable,
doesn't he?
CHARLES.
Yes.
(Beat. On the verge of something, then, quietly:)
I don't know who you've been talking to but
I *do* know my subject.
... I really do.
(Lights. Toby, Stempel, Freedman, Enright enter, their scenes crossing before sorting themselves out.)
STEMPEL.
Toby!
FREEDMAN.
Dan!
TOBY.
I'm going to the store.

FREEDMAN.
Dan, we have to talk.
STEMPEL.
You have to listen!
I'm such an idiot!
ENRIGHT.
Christ, Al, you're not going to strike up
your end-of-the-world number, are you?
Because I need coffee.
FREEDMAN.
Dan —
(They exit.)
STEMPEL.
The store can wait.
TOBY.
We need bread,
we need soda,
mama's coming back with the baby in —
STEMPEL.
That can *wait — listen — !*
The most amazing thing ...
I was rummaging through the credenza
— acres and acres of *struhlkes* —
You keep house like the *Collier* brothers
but I will never again berate you for it
because I found *this!*
(He shows a photostat sheet.)
I thought it was lost —
irretrievable, I thought,
all of a sudden
I move aside some precious keepsakes
all this crap
and *voilà!*
(Beat. Toby not responding.)
Toby?
TOBY.
I have to get to the store now.
Later there are crowds.

When there are crowds, I can't —
STEMPEL.
No — no — no —
you *must* listen — you don't understand what this *is* —
That time on the show when I got an advance —
Well
you know me — my *mishegas* —
I made a *photostat* of the check.
On the check I made a no*ta*tion:
Advance on Future Winnings!"
Do you *see?*
(No response.)
Toby?
I show this check
and this time they will have to believe me
because this time
it's not *me,*
it's a piece of *paper.*
Do you understand?
TOBY.
... Mama's coming back with the baby
in half-an-hour.
She can't stay;
if you have to go out,
Mrs. Abresch upstairs will —
STEMPEL.
Don't do this!
... Look,
I know this has been difficult.
I know life of late
has been the thing after terrible
but I'm just saying please *listen.*
It's not like I'm asking something *hard*
like you should *love* me or something
just that just that
TOBY.
You think I don't

STEMPEL.
Just that you *listen* when I tell you —
TOBY.
You don't think I —
STEMPEL.
This is good news!
TOBY.   *(Shut eyes; hands over ears.)*
Please! God! No more good news!
(Pause. Stempel goes to her; she turns from him. He almost touches her, hesitates, does, gently.)
STEMPEL.
I
Yes, I
know.
But I will say this
and it will be over
and then
whatever our life is
we can have it
— because it isn't this.
But please
just for now
try, be happy.
TOBY.
... Make sure you're here
when mama comes with the baby.
(She exits.)
STEMPEL.
Toby ...
(Meanwhile, by some stunning directorial stratagem, Enright and Freedman have re-entered unobtrusively.)
ENRIGHT.
... He's a madman; everyone knows he's a madman.
FREEDMAN.
I think they're beginning to doubt his insanity.
(Beat.)
STEMPEL.
THIS IS *GOOD!*

FREEDMAN.
... Dan?
ENRIGHT.
SHIT!
(Quick out on Stempel.)
What kind of world do we live in
that people *want* to talk to Herb *Stempel?*
FREEDMAN.
Please lower your voice.
There are people in the hallway with subpoenas.
ENRIGHT.
I don't give a damn.
FREEDMAN.
Look —
I know you're feeling
very vulnerable right now
but still we have to —
ENRIGHT.
Vulnerable?
... How, vulnerable?
(Beat.)
FREEDMAN.
Oh, really, please ...
Don't be coy with me ... not now ...
We have been
for a long time
operating on this peculiar kind of luck
... but we screwed up ...
and that seems to be coming to a very scary end
and we are
in every way
vul —
ENRIGHT.
Why?
What have we done?
(Pause.)
FREEDMAN.
Dan —

ENRIGHT.
We've broken no law —
what have we done?
(Beat.)
FREEDMAN.
Look —
ENRIGHT.
Violated some principle?
A principle that finds expression
in not a single statute
or or edict
or regulation?
That is at best a *perception* of *wrongdoing*
and I *control* the perceptions?
FREEDMAN.
Um ... Dan ...
ENRIGHT.
Do you see, Al?
Do you understand?
This investigation is going to collapse.
It is going to collapse
from a lack of inner *necessity*.
FREEDMAN.
I think you've lost your mind, so listen to me —
ENRIGHT.
No. *You.*
In the first place, we have done nothing wrong.
In the second place, we have done it in *utmost* secrecy.
Third, we have performed a fa —
a very great and delicate favor for people of enormous pow —
sponsors, a *network* —
enormously powerful people:
We have managed to inform them of everything
without *in any way* compromising their ignorance.
A certain gratitude comes with that,
certain protections —
Has almost everyone gone along with us till now?
Did *legions* of carpenters and *mothers* and shoemakers

— people who had done absolutely nothing illegal *till then* —
march into that grand jury idiocy
and politely perjure themselves
as they were instructed to do?
FREEDMAN.
Explain how this constitutes a defense —
ENRIGHT.
Do you think, what, I don't understand people anymore?
Do you think I've lost my touch or something?
Jesus, Al, you're my partner,
my *friend* —
don't you believe in *anything*?
FREEDMAN. *(Quietly.)*
I believe in little pieces of paper
with writing on them.
(Beat. Almost wistful.)
Danny,
I have no other talents —
could you at least have the courtesy
to panic along with me?
Stempel has that check.
He will show them that check.
A check drawn against winnings
that were not yet won.
Face it, Dan:
What can that possible *mean?*
ENRIGHT.
... Give me a minute.
(Lights. Chord. Title: To Congress. Stempel appears on one side of stage with statement in hand.)
CONGRESSMAN. *(V.O.)*
Mr. Stempel,
you may make your statement.
STEMPEL.
Thank you.
First, I would like to say how honored
and excited I am to be addressing at last
this august body.

While there is nothing new in what I say,
I am privileged to have my remarks attested to
by the annotated document you have before you,
which will serve to authenticate and render irrefutable
my testimony.
I was coached for every one of my appearances
on the *Twenty-One* program,
both as to content and performance
by Mr. Dan Enright.
(Enright appears on other side of stage, casually sits, lights cigarette.)
My grooming on the show
was not my own
and the only answers I gave
that accurately represented my body of knowledge
were the ones
that I got right.
But even these
were superfluously given to me in advance.
You've asked me what I know about my successor.
while I was not involved in his coaching sessions,
I was let know when I would lose
and how could that be known unless it was ascertained
that he would win. Ipso facto.
I am certain that if you call him before you,
it will only serve to make
my true remarks truer.
In any event,
you have that check
in addition to my Bible oath.
(Chord. Title: To the Press. Lights fuller on Enright.)
ENRIGHT.
Yes, it's true,
I did give Mr. Stempel that money.
STEMPEL.
Once again, I want to thank you
both implicitly and explicitly.
ENRIGHT.
But I wouldn't call it an advance.

STEMPEL.
Thank you.
ENRIGHT.
You see, Mr. Stempel was threatening to quit the show while he was still winning.
STEMPEL.
Thank you so much.
(He grins. Freeze.)
ENRIGHT.
I thought that would be unfair to the viewers
— and the only way to appease him was money.
He was enormously interested in money.
As for these accusations,
I believe they have two sources:
First,
an irrational hatred for Charles Van Doren —
Mr. Stempel has a long history under psychoanalytic care, by the way
— oh, I hope that's off the record.
Second
— and this is difficult for me —
Mr. Stempel's father died
when Mr. Stempel was just a boy.
He came to look upon me —
as a sort of replacement father figure
and ... well ...
I'm sure you're all familiar
with the idea of the "Oedipal Complex" ...
(Stempel unfreezes, his smile fades. Stempel and Enright turn to face each other. Chord. Appearing as they speak:)
JACK BARRY.
At *Twenty-One* we vehemently deny
GERITOL SPONSOR.
At Geritol we are shocked by the very idea that
NETWORK REP.
At NBC and *The Today Show*, we heartily support
GERITOL SPONSOR.
Geritol does not believe in hoodwinking the public

NETWORK REP.
Mr. Van Doren is as honest as his face
JACK BARRY.
We have never violated your trust
NETWORK REP.
Why, the Harris Committee has never even felt the need to ask Mr. Van Doren to testify, so satisfied are they with
DORIS.
Whenever I saw Mr. Van Doren at NBC,
he was nice as nice can be
JACK BARRY.
We have never violated your faith in us
NETWORK REP.
At NBC we counsel our loyal viewers to remember the ancient adage:
GERITOL SPONSOR.
Geritol believes in giving old people *vim*
NETWORK REP.
"Just because your house is being devoured,
it doesn't mean you're a termite."
JACK BARRY.
We have never violated the hope you place in us
DORIS.
While Mr. *Stempel* never looked me in the eye
JACK BARRY.
And we never will
GERITOL SPONSOR.
A pathological liar may be pitied
but he must never be believed.
Good evening.
(Charles in his office at Columbia. Midnight. A radio plays.)
RADIO.   *(V.O.)*
... has not yet responded personally to the charges
although a *Today Show* spokesman this evening said that Mr.
        Van Doren is completely
(Charles flicks off the switch. He picks up a book, tries to read. Turns radio back on.)

... Meanwhile Mr. Van Doren has continued to teach his
(Charles quickly turns to another station. V.O.)
... while Dave Garroway has given his personal assurance that his *Today Show* colleague is as
(Charles turns station again. V.O.)
... *Twenty-One* producer Dan Enright meanwhile is
(Charles starts flicking among stations; it has a grizzly fascination for him, an inundating horror he's almost exhausted enough to enjoy. Station babble. V.O.)
... be allowed to continue on *The Today Show* while ... son of Mark Van Doren, Pulitzer Prize-winning author of ... was implicated by ... although Mr. Stempel's charges were effectively refuted by ... he has, surprisingly, remained silent on the issue and ...
(Charles turns off radio. He goes to book. Closes it. He picks up a piece of paper on which something is scrawled, considers it, puts it down, picks it up again, puts it down. Once more. Then he takes up book again and reads. Stempel appears at doorway. A moment. Stempel just stares at Charles's back for a time. Much of this scene has an eerie, dislocated, middle-of-the-night quality.)
STEMPEL.   *(Softly.)*
Mr. Van Doren?
(Charles is a little startled to hear anyone at this hour; turns. The lights are dim, not an instant recognition.)
CHARLES.
Yes?
Who's there?
STEMPEL.
Remember me?
(Charles looks at him. Long pause.)
CHARLES.
You look different.
STEMPEL.
It's my clothes.
CHARLES.
Yes; they —

STEMPEL.
— fit.
(Beat.)
CHARLES.
What are you doing here?
STEMPEL.
I know, it's peculiar.
I couldn't sleep.
CHARLES.
Take a pill.
STEMPEL.
In my system these days
all pills become amphetamines.
I took a walk.
CHARLES.
You live in Brooklyn.
STEMPEL.
Queens.
CHARLES.
This is Morningside Heights.
STEMPEL.
I got on a subway.
I didn't even know where to.
I got off here.
There's a sign on the path:
"This Way to the Smartest Man in the World."
I figured — that's you?
CHARLES.
My students put that up last year.
STEMPEL.
It's still there.
I followed the sign
and here you are.
Midnight.
You *lu*cubrate.
That means works deep into the —
CHARLES.
I know what it means.

STEMPEL.
I need to talk to somebody.
CHARLES.
And you choose me?
STEMPEL.
Did you read the papers?
Mr. Enright
he's saying
he's telling the press
— lies — !
that he was a *father* figure
that I had to over*throw* him
that that
... okay, maybe there's something *to* it
it's a theme I should explore
but it's not what happened!
CHARLES.
You already took a good slice out of me
in front of that committee,
have you come back to collect the rest?
STEMPEL.
No one believes me.
Nobody will believe me until you talk.
CHARLES.   *(On "talk.")*
Look —
I can understand that you'd hate me —
STEMPEL.
What?
CHARLES.
but it's not going to get you anywhere to
STEMPEL.
I don't even *know* you.
Why do you think I hate you —
because people say so?
They also say
you know the answers to
fifteen-thousand obscure questions,

and you're still listening to people?
CHARLES.
Why else would you be here — if you didn't —
STEMPEL. *(Overlaps.)*
You're *incidental!*
CHARLES.
Oh — *please* — don't —
STEMPEL. *(Continuous.)*
Look
you you
drive in your car
there's tumbleweed or something on the road
you drive *over* it
your mind is not on that
your mind is on your *destination* —
until *you* talk nobody will listen to *me* and —
CHARLES. *(Over from "Drive over it.")*
Whatever may be going on with you,
hating me, blaming me is not going to help,
all it can do is make it even —
STEMPEL.
WHY DOES THIS HAVE TO BE ABOUT *YOU?*
Why can't it be about ME?
Am I your *shadow?*
Is my life
some sort of some
sort of *afterthought* to yours?
(Pause.)
CHARLES. *(Quiet.)*
No ...
STEMPEL.
I'm
No. Yes. No.
I'm sorry.
Forgive me.
I'm often not so shrill.
I haven't slept....

I had that *check*.
I go announce it and think,
now things will sort themselves out.
I come back home —
No one —
Everyone —
*No*thing —
People who once thought me off-balance
now find I'm psychotic.
And then Mr. Enright is so helpful
as to explain to the world
the specific *kind* of lunatic I am ...
All night
I'm wandering through the streets like a spook,
looking for an interlocutor ...
You're the only one I could think to talk to
who has to believe me ...
Forgive me.
I'm trespassing.
If I start walking home now
maybe by the time I arrive
I'll be awake with the rest of the people.
CHARLES.
Where are you going?
STEMPEL.
I'm leaving
... Why? Don't you want me to leave?
CHARLES.
I
Yes, I must.
STEMPEL. *(Going.)*
Then good night.
CHARLES.
I don't sleep either.
STEMPEL.
That's because —
CHARLES.
Because I've been accused —

that's all.
I've been accused and it's everywhere ...
I've stayed in this office
the last two nights —
made excuses to my wife
entombed myself here
and I wait.
For the catastrophe that never completely happens.
So I
teach my classes like someone unrecognizable.
Sleep just long enough to wake in a sweat
and try to replace the world with these books
... It doesn't work.
I can't get through them.
And the world keeps coming in anyway.
You're right, you know —
I finally read some of the letters —
everyone *does* believe me.
STEMPEL.
I know.
CHARLES.
It's amazing — it's a riot!
They believe me — what a thing!
STEMPEL.
Yes.
CHARLES.
It's ... horrible.
I want this part of my life to be over
but I'm too scared to say what I have to
to bring it to an end.
STEMPEL.
What are you going to tell them when they call you?
What will you say when —
CHARLES. *(Overlaps.)*
I don't think they're going to call me.
I don't think they want to —
STEMPEL. *(Overlaps.)*
It doesn't have to be their decision!

You can *go* before them, you can *choose* to —
CHARLES.
I know.
STEMPEL.
for *someone* to *glean* the right values
to bring this part of our
of your life to an end — you *want* that —
CHARLES.
Yes.
STEMPEL.
Then will you —
CHARLES.
I don't know.
STEMPEL.
But —
CHARLES.
I don't know.
STEMPEL.
But you've just told me — you've told *me*.
CHARLES.
We're two people alone in a room here.
STEMPEL.   *(Quiet, deflated.)*
... Oh ... oh ...
Well then
that's that ...
(A moment. Should he stay? Go? Dissatisfied. Then:)
What were you reading when I came in?
CHARLES.
... Why?
STEMPEL.
I bet I've read it, too.
CHARLES.
... Creve-Couer. For my class in —
STEMPEL.   *(Overlaps.)*
I knew it — I read him!
Creve-Coeur — Henry Adams — Ben Franklin — your father —
all the Americans.

I bet I remember it better than you.
I know more things than you do.
Because I never forget anything.
I wish I could.
We might discuss our reading sometime
except it would be absurd.
CHARLES.
Yes.
(Beat.)
STEMPEL.
I *will* walk, I think —
I'm glad we talked.
CHARLES.   *(A little cordial, formal.)*
So am I.
STEMPEL.
... Good luck to you.
CHARLES.
Good luck to *you.*
STEMPEL.
Tell the truth.
(Stempel exits. A moment. Charles picks up the page he crumpled at the beginning of the scene.)
CHARLES.   *(Reads.)*
"Respectfully request you read following statement into the record of the proceedings before your committee, quote: 'Mr. Van Doren has made himself available to members of the committee's staff. He is available to speak to the committee directly.'" ...
(He looks at it, seems about to tear it in two. Then, he picks up a pen and hastily scrawls on it.)
... Charles Van Doren.
(Lights. Projection: Charles before Committee. Under sound, the hearing assembles. Charles puts on his jacket and walks U. to where the Congresspeople take their places. D., Stempel and Toby are seated. Charles shakes hand of committee head and takes his seat. When he does he joins the recorded sound which fades out leaving just him speaking live.)

CONGRESSMAN ONE.
Mr. Van Doren:
You may make your statement.
CHARLES.
Thank you.
I would give almost everything I have
to reverse the course of my life in the last few years.
I cannot take back one word or action;
the past does not change for anyone.
But at least I can learn from the past.
I have learned a lot in these years.
I've learned a lot about life.
I've learned a lot about myself,
and about good and evil.
They are not always what they appear to be.
I was involved
deeply involved
in a deception.
I've been acting a role, it seems,
not just the last few years —
I've been acting a role for ten or fifteen years,
maybe all my life.
I don't ask for forgiveness —
forgiveness would not be appropriate.
I hope someday to earn it.
I have a long way to go
but I am sorry.
I have deceived my friends
and I had millions of them.
(Pause.)
STEMPEL.
And now it comes ...
CONGRESSMAN ONE.
Mr. Van Doren —
CONGRESSMAN TWO.
Mr. Van Doren —
(Beat. Lights on five Congressmen.)

CONGRESSMAN ONE.
Mr. Van Doren,
the soul-searching fortitude
that is displayed
in your statement —
CONGRESSMAN THREE.
Mr. Van Doren.
There is so much good
in the worst of us
and so much bad
in the best of us —
CONGRESSMAN TWO.
I have listened
to many witnesses,
Mr. Van Doren,
but yours is the most soul-searching confession
I think I have heard.
CONGRESSMAN FOUR.
Mr. Van Doren,
the American people are against corruption
but they are for forgiveness.
CONGRESSMAN TWO.
Mr. Van Doren.
CONGRESSMAN FIVE.   *(Overlapped.)*
Mr. Van Doren.
CONGRESSMAN ONE.
Mr. Van Doren,
the measure of a man
is best taken not when he's aloft
but when he's returned to human reach
CONGRESSMAN THREE.
To be a man
is to fall.
CONGRESSMAN FIVE.
How can we look at you
and not recognize a mirror?
CONGRESSMAN ONE.
To tell the truth

is a hard thing
but the only thing
CONGRESSMAN FOUR.
What you have been to people
CONGRESSMAN THREE.
What people have asked you to be
CONGRESSMAN TWO.
No man should bear the burden
CONGRESSMAN FIVE.
No man can possibly
CONGRESSMAN TWO.
Only one man ever has
CONGRESSMAN FOUR.
The world today
CONGRESSMAN FIVE.
This country
CONGRESSMAN THREE.
This abundant
CONGRESSMAN TWO.
This perilous country
CONGRESSMAN ONE.
With so much on offer
CONGRESSMAN TWO.
With everything on offer
CONGRESSMAN FOUR.
With everything on offer to you
CONGRESSMAN TWO.
A man of your talents
CONGRESSMAN FIVE.
A man of your appeal
CONGRESSMAN THREE.
This story was inevitable
CONGRESSMAN TWO.
This story was undeniable
CONGRESSMAN ONE.
This story was waiting for its hero
CONGRESSMAN FIVE.
The bravery you've shown today

CONGRESSMAN THREE.
The gallantry you've shown
CONGRESSMAN FOUR.
God bless you for this
CONGRESSMAN TWO.
God bless you
CONGRESSMAN FIVE.
May God bless you, Mr. Van Doren
CONGRESSMAN ONE.
God be with you
and thank you
(The knock of a gavel. Congressmen shake hands, gather papers, etc., and exit. A moment. Toby rises to go. Charles and Stempel remain seated.)
TOBY.
Herb...?
(Beat. He looks at her. Very softly, he starts to laugh. The laughter grows in volume and intensity. Soon, Charles is laughing, too. This goes on for quite a while. Slowly, Charles' voice fades and the light narrows in on Stempel whose laughter turns dry, then barely audible, then silent. Fade out. Enright's office. Enright and Freedman. Enright rummages through box.)
ENRIGHT.
Do you want a ceremonial cup
from the Kiwanis?
I think it's started to oxidize.
FREEDMAN.
I'm fine.
(Offstage, Barry: "Goddamn it!")
ENRIGHT.
The crap in here —
(Barry enters.)
BARRY.
Danny, where's my putter?
ENRIGHT.
I don't know, Jack.
BARRY.
I keep it behind the wet bar,

it's always there, it's not there,
where is it?
Al?
FREEDMAN.
I'm sorry, Jack.
BARRY. *(Exiting.)*
Why the hell can't I find my putter?
I didn't lie!
I didn't cheat!
(He's gone.)
ENRIGHT.
Well, you know, he *didn't*.
(He sits, drinks. Freedman packs one final item, looks around.)
FREEDMAN.
That's about it, I guess....
So.
Dan.
What do we do now?
ENRIGHT.
U-u-u-u-u-h-h ...
I can't say at the moment.
This has been something of a setback.
(Beat.)
Luckily, my reputation's intact.
(Beat.)
FREEDMAN.
Jeez, you know I'm standing here,
and there's so much I wish I could stop thinking about.
I'd like not to think about what we've done.
I would *love*
not to be wondering why it is
I've been indicted
and you haven't.
And I keep trying
but I can't remember —
I can't picture it —
can you?

ENRIGHT.
What's that?
FREEDMAN.
What was life like *before* television?
(Lights.)
ENRIGHT. *(Out.)*
Coda:
Charles goes home.
(As the stage empties. Title: What Was Life Like Before Television? West Cornwall. A clearing. Charles and Mark enter, carrying a wood table and benches. They scope out the area, find a place, set up the furniture.)
MARK.
There!
I think this is a nice spot.
CHARLES.
Yes.
It was my favorite when I was young.
Bugs.
MARK.
Hm?
CHARLES.
There are bugs.
MARK.
There would be bugs wherever.
Outdoors.
CHARLES.
It'll be worse with the food.
(Beat.)
Shall I get the food?
MARK.
No.
No one will be here for half-an-hour yet.
CHARLES.
Okay.
(Beat.)
Let's go back in, then.

MARK.
Let's stay out a bit.
CHARLES.
And do what?
I mean why?
MARK.
We can sit.
(Beat.)
CHARLES.
Fine.
(Beat.)
Who's coming.
MARK.
Friends.
CHARLES.
... Maybe I won't stay.
MARK.
These are people you like.
These are people you've always liked.
CHARLES.
Even so.
MARK.
It's a gathering.
CHARLES.
That doesn't *cheer* ...
Oh.
All right.
MARK.
You can't —
CHARLES.
I know.
MARK.
It just won't *work* to —
CHARLES.
Got it, yes, I've agreed.
MARK.
Good.
(Beat.)

I think this is the best season here.
CHARLES.   *(Distantly.)*
... Yes ... the leaves ... colors.
MARK.
There's so little to take care of, now.
Nothing to mow, nothing you have to cut back —
CHARLES.
Then ... what have you been doing here?
MARK.
Doing? ...
Nothing, really, I guess.
There are no events here at all, really,
and we hardly ever go into the city any more.
Your mother and I have become devoted to the monotony
of this place.
It seems the less that happens
the more we experience
because it comes at us
in such small portions.
It's good for poets, I think.
It does nothing for conversation
but it pleases us.
CHARLES.
Maybe this.
Find some house somewhere
all covered over.
Sit in it.
Read.
That might be —
MARK.
I doubt it's possible for you.
CHARLES.
You do it —
MARK.
I was born in the last century,
it's natural to me;
but that sort of rhythm of things
is over now, I think.

You have to live in your own time
... It will catch up to you anyway ...
CHARLES.
Not even this, then ...
MARK.
... I *have* been doing something;
I've been making lists.
CHARLES.
Lists?
What of?
MARK.
Last week
I made a list of all the poems
I wanted to write for the rest of my life.
CHARLES.
Morbid little list.
MARK.
These were things I would celebrate.
CHARLES.
Oh ...
You must have *needed* a list like that around —
MARK. *(Overlapped.)*
It went on forever, it was impossible.
And the funny part was
when I finally finished the list
I realized it was a poem.
Perhaps you'll break with tradition and read it.
CHARLES.
Perhaps I will.
(Beat.)
MARK.
Talk to me, Charlie.
CHARLES.
About what.
MARK.
About anything.
Just talk to me
before the people start arriving

and we have to get cordial.
CHARLES.
There's no need —
MARK.
I want —
CHARLES.   *(Continuous.)*
I mean, "to talk"
in that *significant* way.
What has to be said
has been said,
done.
I mean, this isn't like a disease or something —
MARK.
I know that —
CHARLES.
No, except in a way of course it *is* like a disease.
When you've got it
in some secret, terrible way
people don't want you to be rid of it
because it's such a foolproof topic, you know,
something they can feed off
for conversation.
I'm tired of all the talk in the world:
talk is a parasite.
I only speak nonsense, anyway.
(Beat.)
I mean, I have nothing to say.
(Pause.)
Two of my students
... did you hear this? ...
They collected something like six-hundred signatures
on a petition demanding my re-instatement.
There was a rally:
five-hundred showed up.
MARK.
The respect of your students —
CHARLES.
Stop.

(Pause.)
In the middle of it,
this guy called out from a dorm room,
"Hey, Charlie's in the quad
handing out the answers to the Comparative Lit final."
... One group over on the side of things
started to applaud him
then others — cheering ...
Those are people I might like to know.
(Beat.)
MARK.
Columbia isn't the world —
CHARLES.
Of course it is.
(Beat.)
Can we go?
I don't like this spot.
MARK.
You just said you loved it.
CHARLES.
Not any more.
(Beat.)
I don't feel anything any more.
(Beat.)
MARK.
I don't believe you Charlie.
CHARLES.
No, you're right.
One thing:
shame.
The simplest things are filled with it
... waking up ...
And it never goes away,
not for a second.
It's the only thing I can depend on, really:
this feeling of being ashamed.
(Beat.)
Or else I just cry well in public.

MARK.
I'd like to help you, Charlie.
CHARLES.
But you can't.
You of all people.
We're opposites, you and I;
you love the world
and I think I've come to hate it.
MARK.
Don't say that to me.
CHARLES.
But it's true!
I've betrayed
everything
and
I ... hate it
I hate
the sound of my own voice.
I wish I never had to speak
another word —
all the words have broken in me.
I want ... to be rid of them,
if I could just be rid of them
but it's not possible.
I started out as nothing much
and then I became *this*
and now it's the only thing I ever can be.
I want to start over
but how
I don't know how
I can't imagine where
I
can't imagine it ... I ... can't ... I ...
(*He's in tears now. Mark holds him; he allows it. A long moment.*)
MARK.
Charlie, you're right.
The world's a terrible place
... and the worst things seem to happen toward the end ...

But
the list ... you know ...
So many ... things ...
(Pause.)
Tell me what to say, Charlie.
I can't have got to this point
and have nothing useful to say.
(Beat.)
CHARLES.
I'm sorry for what I've done to you.
MARK.
...Thank you for that,
but you're mine.
(Beat.)
CHARLES.
I think I do want to go in now —
MARK.
Charlie —
CHARLES.
Look
this is
I'm fine
MARK.
Why don't you —
CHARLES.
You've cut down that tree.
(Beat.)
MARK.
What?
CHARLES.
I just noticed it —
that old tree is gone.
MARK.
Oh.

to.

ng up the plumbing.

CHARLES.
I thought so.
MARK.
I know.
(Beat.)
CHARLES.
That was a strange
some
an exotic tree, wasn't it?
A shame to cut it down.
What was that tree called?
MARK.
An oak.
CHARLES.
... I don't know the name of the commonest
MARK.
But you grew up in the middle of it all.
CHARLES.
When you grow up in the middle of it,
you don't have to know the names,
you can just point ...
So that was an oak.
I noticed it was missing, though.
MARK.
Yes.
CHARLES.
... That one over there, then,
that must be another oak, yes?
MARK.
That's a maple.
CHARLES.
Oh ... it looks the same as —
MARK.
And next to it is a cedar.
... and a paper birch, tamarack ... black birch ... black pine ...
CHARLES.
Hm.
Maple, cedar, paper birch, tamarack, black birch, black pine —

MARK.
You're a quick study.
CHARLES.
I know that.
Maple, cedar, tamarack, paper birch —
MARK.
paper birch, tamarack —
CHARLES.
paper birch, tamarack, black birch ... black pine.
MARK.
That's it.
(Beat.)
CHARLES.
The names.
MARK.
Yes.
(Beat.)
CHARLES.
... That one over there?
MARK.
Charlie,
why don't you look in the branches?
I think you can figure it out for yourself.
CHARLES.
Oh!
Right.
Apple.
... And that's another tamarack, isn't it?
MARK.
Yes.
(Lights begin slowly to fade.)
CHARLES.
... and a paper birch
another cedar
MARK.
Yes
CHARLES.
and a maple

and another
... and a black birch
and a row of them
and a tamarack
a black pine
another maple
another cedar
and a ...
(Fade out.)

End of Play

PROPERTY LIST

Question cards (ENRIGHT)
Shiny suit (ENRIGHT)
Watch (STEMPEL)
Headphones (STEMPEL)
Letter (SPONSOR)
Pile of letters (SPONSOR)
Personal cards on Charles (ENRIGHT)
Cigarettes, lit (CORSO, CHARLES, ENRIGHT)
Drinks (ENRIGHT)
Coffee (DORIS)
Paper and pen (CHARLES)
Tape recorder (ENRIGHT)
Papers (INVESTIGATOR)
Watch (CHARLES)
Photostat sheet (STEMPEL)
Book (CHARLES)
Papers (CONGRESSMEN)
Box of office momentos (ENRIGHT)
Furniture pieces (MARK, CHARLES)

SOUND EFFECTS

Watch ticking
Phone ringing

TODAY'S HOTTEST NEW PLAYS

❑ **MOLLY SWEENEY by Brian Friel, Tony Award-Winning Author of *Dancing at Lughnasa*.** Told in the form of monologues by three related characters, *Molly Sweeney* is mellifluous, Irish storytelling at its dramatic best. Blind since birth, Molly recounts the effects of an eye operation that was intended to restore her sight but which has unexpected and tragic consequences. "Brian Friel has been recognized as Ireland's greatest living playwright. *Molly Sweeney* confirms that Mr. Friel still writes like a dream. Rich with rapturous poetry and the music of rising and falling emotions...Rarely has Mr. Friel written with such intoxicating specificity about scents, colors and contours." - *New York Times*. [2M, 1W]

❑ **SWINGING ON A STAR (The Johnny Burke Musical) by Michael Leeds. 1996 Tony Award Nominee for Best Musical.** The fabulous songs of Johnny Burke are perfectly represented here in a series of scenes jumping from a 1920s Chicago speakeasy to a World War II USO Show and on through the romantic high jinks of the Bob Hope/Bing Crosby "Road Movies." Musical numbers include such favorites as "Pennies from Heaven," "Misty," "Ain't It a Shame About Mame," "Like Someone in Love," and, of course, the Academy Award winning title song, "Swinging on a Star." "A WINNER. YOU'LL HAVE A BALL!" - *New York Post*. "A dazzling, toe-tapping, finger-snapping delight!" - *ABC Radio Network*. "Johnny Burke wrote his songs with moonbeams!" - *New York Times*. [3M, 4W]

❑ **THE MONOGAMIST by Christopher Kyle.** Infidelity and mid-life anxiety force a forty-something poet to reevaluate his 60s values in a late 80s world. "THE BEST COMEDY OF THE SEASON. Trenchant, dark and jagged. Newcomer Christopher Kyle is a playwright whose social satire comes with a nasty, ripping edge - Molière by way of Joe Orton." - *Variety*. "By far the most stimulating playwright I've encountered in many a buffaloed moon." - *New York Magazine*. "Smart, funny, articulate and wisely touched with rue...the script radiates a bright, bold energy." - *The Village Voice*. [2M, 3W]

❑ **DURANG/DURANG by Christopher Durang.** These cutting parodies of *The Glass Menagerie* and *A Lie of the Mind*, along with the other short plays in the collection, prove once and for all that Christopher Durang is our theater's unequivocal master of outrageous comedy. "The fine art of parody has returned to theater in a production you can sink your teeth and mind into, while also laughing like an idiot." - *New York Times*. "If you need a break from serious drama, the place to go is Christopher Durang's silly, funny, over-the-top sketches." - *TheatreWeek*. [3M, 4W, flexible casting]

DRAMATISTS PLAY SERVICE, INC.
440 Park Avenue South, New York, New York 10016 212-683-8960 Fax 212-213-1539

TODAY'S HOTTEST NEW PLAYS

❏ **THREE VIEWINGS by Jeffrey Hatcher.** Three comic-dramatic monologues, set in a midwestern funeral parlor, interweave as they explore the ways we grieve, remember, and move on. *"Finally, what we have been waiting for: a new, true, idiosyncratic voice in the theater. And don't tell me you hate monologues; you can't hate them more than I do. But these are much more: windows into the deep of each speaker's fascinating, paradoxical, unique soul, and windows out into a gallery of surrounding people, into hilarious and horrific coincidences and conjunctions, into the whole dirty but irresistible business of living in this damnable but spellbinding place we presume to call the world."* - New York Magazine. [1M, 2W]

❏ **HAVING OUR SAY by Emily Mann.** The Delany Sisters' Bestselling Memoir is now one of Broadway's Best-Loved Plays! Having lived over one hundred years apiece, Bessie and Sadie Delany have plenty to say, and their story is not simply African-American history or women's history...it is our history as a nation. *"The most provocative and entertaining family play to reach Broadway in a long time."* - New York Times. *"Fascinating, marvelous, moving and forceful."* - Associated Press. [2W]

❏ **THE YOUNG MAN FROM ATLANTA Winner of the 1995 Pulitzer Prize. by Horton Foote.** An older couple attempts to recover from the suicide death of their only son, but the menacing truth of why he died, and what a certain Young Man from Atlanta had to do with it, keeps them from the peace they so desperately need. *"Foote ladles on character and period nuances with a density unparalleled in any living playwright."* - NY Newsday. [5M, 4W]

❏ **SIMPATICO by Sam Shepard.** Years ago, two men organized a horse racing scam. Now, years later, the plot backfires against the ringleader when his partner decides to come out of hiding. *"Mr. Shepard writing at his distinctive, savage best."* - New York Times. [3M, 3W]

❏ **MOONLIGHT by Harold Pinter.** The love-hate relationship between a dying man and his family is the subject of Harold Pinter's first full-length play since *Betrayal*. *"Pinter works the language as a master pianist works the keyboard."* - New York Post. [4M, 2W, 1G]

❏ **SYLVIA by A.R. Gurney.** This romantic comedy, the funniest to come along in years, tells the story of a twenty-two year old marriage on the rocks, and of Sylvia, the dog who turns it all around. *"A delicious and dizzy new comedy."* - New York Times. *"FETCHING! I hope it runs longer than Cats!"* - New York Daily News. [2M, 2W]

DRAMATISTS PLAY SERVICE, INC.
440 Park Avenue South, New York, New York 10016   212-683-8960   Fax 212-213-1539